The Carnivore Bible

Strengthen Your Health and Muscles with 1200 Days of Succulent and Effortless Meat Recipes | Meal Plan Against High Cholesterol Included

Jasper Wilder

Table of Contents

Chapter 1: Introduction to the Carnivore Diet — 12

What is the Carnivore Diet? — 14

Benefits of the Carnivore Diet — 14

- Lowers Blood Sugar Levels — 15
- Weight Loss — 15
- Fewer Digestive Issues — 15
- May Improve Mental Clarity — 15
- Decreases Inflammation — 16
- Could Prevent the Loss of Testosterone — 16
- Helps Heart Health — 16

Challenges of the Carnivore Diet — 17

- Constipation — 18
- Very Repetitive — 18
- Expensive — 18
- Potential Health Risks — 18

How to Get Started with the Carnivore Diet — 19

- Commit to a Specific Timeframe — 19
- Eat Only Meat — 20
- Drink Mainly Water — 20
- Join a Community of Carnivore Dieters — 20
- Eat Until You are Full — 21
- Remove Temptations — 21
  - List of Foods to Avoid — 21
- Stock Up on Rich and Delicious Carnivore Foods — 22
- Cook Your Meat How You Like It — 23

Do Resistance Training Exercises	23
7-Day Carnivore Diet Food Plan	**24**
Surviving the First Month on the Carnivore Diet	**25**
Get a Blood Test	25
Expect Cravings	26
Try Some Variety	26

Chapter 2: Understanding the Science Behind the Carnivore Diet — 27

The Evolutionary Perspective	**28**
The Evolutionary Basis	**28**
Macronutrient and Micronutrient Considerations	**29**
Macronutrients On Carnivore	30
Micronutrients On Carnivore	30
The Impact of the Carnivore Diet on Health	**31**
Nutrients in Meat Improve Digestion	32
Carnivore Diets Cut Carbs	32
Debunking Common Myths about the Carnivore Diet	**33**
Causes Colon Cancer	33
Causes Scurvy	33
You Need Fiber to Pass out Feces	34
Causes Your Kidneys Harm	34
Causes Global Warming	35
No Phytochemicals	35

Chapter 3: Creating a Healthy and Sustainable Carnivore Lifestyle — 37

Sustainability Considerations	**38**
How to Choose Sustainable Meat Sources	**38**
Choosing the Right Meats and Animal Products	**39**

What Can You Eat on the Carnivore Diet?	39
Golden Rule of the Carnivore Diet	39

Carnivore Diet Food List: What to Eat and What Not to Eat On the Carnivore Diet — 40

Making Good Meat Choices	40
Seafood	41
Organ Meats	41
Pork Skin	41
Eggs	41
Meats to Avoid	41
Most Nutrient Dense Carnivore Foods	42
The Best Ways to Source Carnivore Foods	42

Supplements and Nutritional Considerations — 43

Beef Organs — The Ultimate Multivitamin	44
Electrolytes — No More Carnivore Side Effects	44
Ox Bile — Digest Fat Easier	44
Vitamin C — Difficult to Get from Just Meat	45
Collagen — Heal Your Gut	45
Stearic Acid — Get Your Body to Shape	45

Alternatives to Carnivore Supplements — 46

Sea Salt	46
Beef Liver Crisps	46
Bone Broth	47
Beef Tallow and Suet	47

What Supplements Would You Need to Take? — 47

The Role of Exercise in the Carnivore Lifestyle — 48

Bodybuilding On the Carnivore Diet	49

Strength Training On the Carnivore Diet		50
Endurance Training On the Carnivore Diet		50
Sport-Specific Training On the Carnivore Diet		50

Chapter 4: Carnivore Meal Planning and Preparation — 51

How to Prepare a Carnivore Diet Meal Plan — 51

- Plan to Give all Your Commitment — 52
- Know the Reason for Deciding on the Carnivore Diet — 52
- Be Socially Prepared — 52

Meal Planning 101 — 53

- Standard Meal Plan — 53
- Nose-to-Tail with Dairy Meal Plan — 54
- The Lion Diet Meal Plan — 54
- Carnivore Adjacent Meal Plan — 54

Grocery Shopping for the Carnivore Diet — 55

- Beef — 55
- Seafood & Lamb — 56
- Chicken & Pork — 56
- Organ Meats — 57
- Less Optimal Foods — 57

Simple and Delicious Carnivore Recipes — 58

1. Easy Cheeseburger Pie — 58
2. Carnivore Meatballs with Beef Heart — 60
3. Tartare — 61
4. Egg Pudding — 62

Eating Out and Traveling on the Carnivore Diet — 63

Navigating the American Food Landscape on the Carnivore Diet — 64

Substituting Popular American Foods with Carnivore-Friendly Alternatives — 66

    Replace Burgers with Carnivore Burgers — 66

    Replace French Fries with Carnivore French Fries — 67

    Replace Pizza with Carnivore Pizza — 67

    Replace Ice Cream with Dairy Desserts — 67

Chapter 5: Carnivore Cuisine for Breakfast — 69

Classic Carnivore Breakfasts — 69

    1. Bacon and Eggs — 69

    2. Steak and Eggs — 70

    3. Sausage and Eggs — 72

    4. Ham and Eggs — 73

Creative Carnivore Breakfast Recipes — 74

    1. Breakfast Steak Burrito — 74

    2. Carnivore Omelet — 75

    3. Bacon and Egg Breakfast Salad — 76

    4. Chorizo and Egg Breakfast Bowl — 77

Breakfast Meal Planning and Preparation Tips — 79

    Why is a Nutritious Breakfast So Crucial? — 79

    What is Meal Preparation? — 80

    Benefits of Meal Prepping — 80

    Tips to Help Meal Preparation — 80

        Correctly Combine the Ingredients — 81

        Make Use of the Right Containers — 81

        Choose the Appropriate Ingredients — 81

    How to Meal Prep for the Week — 81

        Food Planning — 81

Get Organized	81
Make Preparations For and Use Leftovers	82
Portion Meals in Advance	82
Modify Your Menu	82
Use the Freezer	83
Bulk Purchases	83
Bulk Cook	83

Quick and Easy Breakfast Ideas for Busy Mornings — 84

1. Carnivore Breakfast Pizza	84
2. Carnivore Breakfast Sandwich	86
3. Keto Carnivore Waffle	87

Tips for Cooking the Perfect Steak or Bacon — 88

A Cold Steak Must Not Be Cooked	88
Avoid Seasoning Your Steak Too Much	89
Choose a Suitable Cooking Oil	89
A Good Pan Should Be Used, and It Should Be Very Hot	89
Avoid Overcooking Your Steak	89
Do Not Be Concerned with the Number of Times You Flip Your Steak	90
Serve the Steak After It Has Rested	90
Serve On a Warm Plate and Cut Against the Grain	90

Chapter 6: Carnivore Recipes — *92*

Chicken — 92

1. Fried Chicken	92
2. Chicken Alfredo	94
3. BBQ Chicken	95
4. Chicken Parmesan	97

5. Roast Chicken … 99

Pork … **100**

　　1. Pork Chops … 100

　　2. Pork Ribs … 101

　　3. Ham … 103

　　4. Bacon … 104

　　5. Sausages … 105

Beef … **108**

　　1. Hamburgers … 108

　　2. Steak … 109

　　3. Roast Beef … 110

　　4. Meatloaf … 112

　　5. Tacos … 113

Lamb … **114**

　　1. Grilled Lamb Chops … 114

　　2. Lamb Roast … 116

　　3. Lamb Kofta … 117

　　4. Lamb Curry … 119

　　5. Lamb Shank … 120

Seafood (Continuation) … **122**

　　1. Fried Shrimp … 122

　　2. Lobster with Butter … 123

　　3. Grilled Fish … 125

　　4. Seafood Paella … 126

　　5. Clam Chowder … 128

Game … **130**

1. Grilled Rabbit — 130
2. Venison Stew — 132
3. Roast Duck — 134
4. Pheasant Bake — 135
5. Wild Boar Chops — 137

Snacks and Salads — **138**

1. French Fries — 138
2. Chicken Salad — 139
3. Chicken Salad — 141
4. Caesar Salad — 142
5. Steak Salad — 144
6. BLT Sandwich — 146
6. Hot Dogs — 147
7. Buffalo Wings — 148
8. Pulled Pork Sandwich — 149

Chapter 7: Meal Planning and Preparation Tips — *151*

How to Plan and Prepare Dinners for the Week — 151

Make Provisions for Flexibility — 152

Doing the Math — 152

The Groundwork: Create a Pantry — 152

Your Fundamental Preparation — 153

How to Cook Perfectly Grilled Steak — 154

Warm Up the Grill — 154

Steaks Should Be Oiled — 154

Season the Steaks — 155

Examine the Temperature — 155

Finish with Butter	155
Clean the Grill	155
Let the Steaks Come to Room Temperature	155
Increase the Taste	155
Steak Doneness Chart	155

Tips for Cooking and Serving Chicken Breasts — 156

Have a Good Understanding of the Chicken Breast	156
Easiest Ways to Cook Chicken Breasts—Including Grilled, Fried, and More	157
Poach Chicken Breasts	157
Grill Chicken Breasts	157
Fry Chicken Breasts	157

Chapter 8: Meal Plans and Menus for the Carnivore Diet — 159

30-Day Carnivore Diet Sample Meal Plans — 159

Week 1	159
Week 2	161
Week 3	162
Week 4	164

Menu Suggestions for Different Occasions — 165

Birthday Menu	165
Thanksgiving Menu	166
Christmas Menu	166
Romantic Dinner Menu	167

Customized Meal Plans for Special Dietary Needs — 167

Meal Plan for Lowering Cholesterol and Balancing Saturated Fats	168
Vegetarian and Vegan Meal Plans	171
Vegan Diet Fundamentals and How to Begin	171

What Can Be Eaten on a Vegan Diet	171
Sample Meal Plan	172

Chapter 9: FAQs about the Carnivore Diet and Lifestyle — 175

How to Overcome Common Challenges — 177

- Adaptation Period Symptoms — 177
- Tips for Staying Motivated and On Track — 178
  - Consuming More Meat — 178
  - Supplements for Electrolyte Support — 178

Chapter 10: Inspiring Stories from Real-Life Carnivore Dieters — 179

- Denise – COVID Survivor — 179
- The Buff Dudes — 180
- Chris and Mark Bell — 180
- Mikhaila and Jordan Peterson — 181

Conclusion and Final Thoughts — 182

- Reflections on the Carnivore Diet and Lifestyle — 182
- The Future of Carnivore Cuisine — 183
- Final Recommendations and Encouragement — 184

Chapter 1: Introduction to the Carnivore Diet

Our modern diet and lifestyle are causing us harm. Modern foods, such as grains, sweets, and unhealthy junk foods, contribute to the chronic inflammation that underpins modern diseases. Furthermore, our poor eating habits fuel inflammation, exacerbated by lack of sleep, inactivity, ongoing stress, and anxiety.

Three out of every five people worldwide die from chronic inflammatory diseases such as stroke, respiratory conditions, obesity, type 2 diabetes, cancer, and various autoimmune disorders. The carnivore diet eliminates the harmful inflammatory agents that cause these illnesses and replaces them with nutrient-dense, whole-food animal products.

The meat-only diet has recently gained popularity on social media, with proponents claiming that this is how humans have survived since the beginning. How true is this, and what else can be learned about the diet?

You've probably already figured out what the Carnivore diet is all about. It is a diet consisting solely of meat and animal products.

This meat-heavy diet is all the rage nowadays, and its use resulted in fewer stomach issues, decreased hunger, increased fat loss, and a slew of other benefits. It recommends eating only meat and avoiding fruits and vegetables. By reducing carbs, you can avoid the health problems caused by a Western diet high in fatty foods and carbs.

While some are correct, you will eventually agree that the Carnivore Diet is debatable. Critics are constantly in the news.

Given how restrictive an all-carnivore lifestyle and pursuit of zero carbs can be, it's not surprising that the carnivore diet has been the subject of much discussion and is harshly criticized by nutritionists and doctors, leading to various headlines.

While going low-carb and avoiding sugars and other common sources of inflammation can benefit health, opponents argue that this diet is not long-term sustainable as it lacks important nutrients like fiber. This makes it difficult to have a balanced nutritional profile without supplementation.

Carnivore dieters frequently refer to historical tribes that ate meat. These societies consumed exceptionally fresh meat regularly, sometimes even raw. They frequently ate the organs, which are high in vital nutrients.

Dieticians argue that the public should not trust the carnivorous diet because it is based on belief rather than scientific reality. No specific studies have been conducted to support its benefits. But what exactly is the carnivore diet, and what else should you know about it?

What is the Carnivore Diet?

The Carnivore diet, as previously stated, excludes all plant foods and is a high-protein Keto diet. It's high in protein and fat, with very few carbohydrates.

It consists of meat, fish, salt, animal fats, eggs, and, occasionally, dairy. Some human carnivores, like animals in this category, eat only meat and avoid dairy and eggs for digestive health. Low-carbohydrate foods such as almonds, avocados, and low-carb vegetables are strictly forbidden.

Because it forbids most food groups, the carnivore diet is considered an elimination diet. Elimination diets are frequently used to treat gastrointestinal issues.

Benefits of the Carnivore Diet

The Carnivore Diet is said to have several health benefits. Although the diet's dependability is heavily contested, there is no denying that many people credit it with being effective. An all-meat diet can help you lose weight, have fewer digestive issues, improve your mental clarity, have higher testosterone levels, have less inflammation, and have less insulin resistance. The Carnivore Diet also has the benefit of being easy to follow.

Lowers Blood Sugar Levels

Because the typical American diet is so high in carbs, we deal with blood sugar spikes and energy loss daily. Blood sugar levels usually balance out because the carnivorous diet prohibits the consumption of sweets. As a result, energy levels are stabilized throughout the day.

Weight Loss

The carnivore diet can be a great ally in losing weight. Long-term studies on how a carnivorous diet may reduce your risk of obesity are not yet available. But almost everyone who follows a carnivorous diet loses weight within a few weeks. When the body's preferred energy source, sugar, is depleted, it uses stored body fat as fuel.

Protein in food has been shown to suppress appetite. While on a carnivorous diet, this may make you less prone to mindless snacking. This practice will almost always keep you from gaining weight.

Fewer Digestive Issues

Fiber, a type of carbohydrate, cannot be digested by the body. It is broken down by stomach bacteria, which can cause bloating and other digestive issues in some people.

Contrary to popular belief, several researchers believe that limiting high-fiber foods like fruits, vegetables, and grains may help some people with digestive issues. According to one study, reducing dietary fiber can help with constipation and its symptoms.

The Carnivore Diet forbids all fiber-containing foods, such as fruits, vegetables, and grains – which may benefit people sensitive to fiber and have digestive issues.

May Improve Mental Clarity

Many Carnivore Diet supporters claim that after following the diet for an extended period, they can think more clearly and concentrate better.

Some supporters compare it to the Keto Diet, in which the body tries to figure out how to fuel the system without carbs.

When you eat more fat and less carbohydrate, your body uses lipids (ketones) instead of glucose and carbohydrates, giving you more energy, focus, and mental clarity.

Although there has been little clinical research on the alleged benefit of mental clarity, many Carnivore Dieters describe data suggesting this may be the case.

Decreases Inflammation

Sugar is a major cause of inflammation. Cutting out sugar and inflammatory vegetables reduces inflammation. Low-carb diets, like carnivorous diets, may help prevent the formation of inflammatory fatty acids.

Could Prevent the Loss of Testosterone

Men's natural testosterone levels begin to decline as they age. According to its supporters, the main benefit of the Carnivore Diet is that it prevents testosterone levels from dropping.

High-protein and high-fat diets have been shown to increase testosterone levels. The high protein and fat intake of the Carnivore Diet can increase testosterone levels, increasing strength, desire, and motivation.

Helps Heart Health

Vitamin K2 is abundant in meat and has been shown to reduce artery calcification, a major cause of heart disease. A high-protein diet may also help lower LDL cholesterol levels.

Some people's cholesterol levels may have risen due to eating much animal meat and fat. However, the overall effect will benefit heart health because of significant reductions in inflammation and insulin surges.

Challenges of the Carnivore Diet

The carnivore diet for autoimmune disease has both benefits and drawbacks. There are risks associated with this restricted dietary plan, but on the other hand, it can potentially restore balance to an unbalanced system.

To begin, it is widely acknowledged that some potential risks include vitamin deficiency due to limited dietary options and digestive issues due to consuming a lot of animal protein. However, many people discover that sticking to such a strict routine over time can be difficult, if not impossible.

Some people are concerned that eliminating fruits and vegetables from our daily diets will result in vitamin deficiencies. Although this is a valid concern, it can be mitigated by eating organic meats. Beef liver is similar to nature's multivitamin.

Another cause for concern is that a low-fiber diet for an extended period may negatively impact the gut microbiota. This is also a legitimate concern, and how to respond will be determined by the individual.

Cooking beef at high temperatures can also produce carcinogenic substances such as advanced glycation end products (AGEs) and heterocyclic amines (HCAs). Cooking beef slowly and at a low temperature reduces the formation of these chemicals.

When deciding whether or not this diet is right for you, it's critical to consider your specific health needs.

It's difficult to overcome these obstacles and embrace independence while adhering to dietary restrictions, but it may be worthwhile as part of any overall health plan.

The carnivore diet may provide impressive results in curing chronic illness while allowing you freedom in what you eat daily with careful monitoring and advice from professionals who understand your circumstances.

It is well known that the limited dietary options make the carnivore diet difficult to maintain over time. That being said, here are some challenges to consider before you begin.

Constipation

The majority of people who follow the diet experience bowel changes early on. It's normal to expect diarrhea at this point, but constipation episodes become more common as fiber is no longer included in this diet. If you suffer from constipation, consider taking a magnesium supplement.

Very Repetitive

If you enjoy trying new foods regularly, the diet's lack of variety may turn you off. Remember, you'll be focusing solely on the meat.

Expensive

Consuming meat and dairy products are not cheap. Due to the high cost of premium meats and organ meat supplements, some people may find it difficult to stick to the diet for an extended period.

Potential Health Risks

Meat consumption has been linked to an increased risk of heart disease, high blood pressure, and high cholesterol. Even though this research frequently results from external circumstances, there may be risks to being a complete carnivore. Some people may have abnormally high iron levels due to eating a piece of red meat. When following this diet, it is critical to consult with a practitioner to assess your iron levels and determine whether you need to donate blood to lower them.

How to Get Started with the Carnivore Diet

Let's go on to the detailed procedure for beginning the carnivorous diet.

Commit to a Specific Timeframe

Don't worry; getting started is easy. This simple eating style requires only a little preparation.

A 1-month challenge is an excellent place to start for most people who want to start eating only meat. For the next 30 days, you will follow the suggested processes, guidelines, and standards. Use this time to assess whether you are experiencing improved health.

Both Drs. Shawn Baker and Ken Berry experimented with a 30-day challenge to transition from a ketogenic to a carnivore diet. They persisted because they were smitten. Goals of 60 to 90 days are more successful for those with better self-control.

Take before-and-after photos, keep a health journal, or monitor these results to see if this diet plan is right for you.

Most people who follow the diet notice the benefits within a few days. However, because there may be some common side effects when switching from your regular diet, it's critical to stick to it for an extended period to allow your body to adjust.

Eat Only Meat

A carnivore diet consists solely of animal meat. This means you should only eat meat and organ meats while on a diet. Plant-based proteins such as peas and beans cannot be consumed.

Every animal-based protein is a recommended type of meat for you to consume. Some people avoid adding dairy fat or protein, such as cream or cheese, while others do.

In addition to the protein, minerals, vitamins, and other nutrients found in meat, the natural saturated and unsaturated animal fat on the meat meets additional daily nutritional needs that your body requires to stay healthy.

Drink Mainly Water

How strict you want to be about following a carnivorous diet is up to you. Most people are advised to drink only water for the first 30 days. This water could be mineral, spring, filtered, or tap water. To add more electrolytes, try adding some salt to your water.

A strict adherent will only eat water and meat. Others could include alcoholic beverages such as coffee, tea, and other fat-containing foods. You're still on the right track if you don't add sugar or other sweeteners to your hot beverages. Avoid drinking hot or cold liquids containing added carbohydrates, such as soda, vegetable juice, energy drinks, and protein drinks.

Join a Community of Carnivore Dieters

Carnivorous diet online communities are fantastic places to exchange ideas and success stories, stay accountable, and find inspiration.

Other thriving carnivore groups have emerged thanks to influential adopters like Jordan Peterson, Paul Saldino, and Amber O'Hearn. Visit them for more information and inspiration!

Dr. Kiltz formed a group called "Mighty Tribe" for this purpose. You are welcome to join for free. World Carnivore Tribe on Facebook is another.

Eat Until You are Full

You should eat enough meat at each meal to satisfy your hunger. Your appetite will fluctuate during the first month. Don't go hungry; eat only what you need.

These options are viable: one meal a day, three meals a day, or intermittent fasting (IF). Snacking should be done with caution in this case.

Your daily schedule determines the frequency with which you eat. If you want, include other health benefits, such as fasting regularly.

If you believe in the biology school of thought, a carnivore breakfast is essential because having protein in the first hour of waking helps to set your body clock.

Eating protein throughout the day and in the evening is a wise decision that will aid in preserving lean muscle mass.

Remove Temptations

Most of us do not eat processed, high-carb foods because we are hungry. We eat it because we are tempted. According to research, as the number of options available grows, so does our ability to make healthy decisions.

Thus, ridding your home of all non-carnivore foods is an important step toward becoming a carnivore. Remove all non-meat products from your pantry.

List of Foods to Avoid

- All fruits: Apples, bananas, berries, tomatoes, avocados, etc.
- All sugars: Added or natural – it doesn't matter. If it's a sweetener, it's off the table, even honey
- All nuts, seeds, and legumes: Almonds, pistachios, peanuts, flax seeds, all beans, etc.
- All vegetables: The usual suspects like broccoli and spinach, along with vegetable broths

- All additives: Processed foods that have nitrates, nitrites, MSG, and oils like lecithin
- All grains: Wheat, rice, buckwheat, quinoa, etc.

Stock Up on Rich and Delicious Carnivore Foods

A good list of foods for a carnivore diet includes:

- Fatty Meat: Ruminant foods, such as fatty steaks like ribeye, short ribs, beef, lamb, and pork belly, are a staple of most carnivore diets.
- Eggs: An ideal ratio of lipids, proteins, and vitamins is abundant in eggs. Boiled eggs can be a great carnivorous snack.
- Organ meats: Nose-to-tail carnivores consume the brain, spleen, pancreas, bone marrow, and bone broth. In addition to bone broth, bone marrow, and cow liver for a staggering amount of essential nutrients such as vitamin K2, B12, and vitamin A.
- Animal fats: You can smother your meats with butter, tallow, and lard since a carnivore diet is a high-fat, low-carb diet.
- Fatty fish: Omega-3 fatty acids are found in king salmon, arctic char, anchovies, and Atlantic mackerel.
- Full-fat dairy: Most people reintroduce some full-fat dairy even though many start as carnivores by removing it. Heavy cream and carnivorous cheeses are acceptable additions, even though milk is sweet and should be avoided.
- Salt: Use a lot of salt in your food to give your body the essential electrolytes it needs. Remember that you need to acquire your salt by adding it to your fresh, natural meals when you cut back on processed foods. You can also increase variety and flavor with a few carnivore diet condiments.

- Seafood: When compared to most animal products, salmon roe, oysters, mussels, shrimp, and crab are excellent providers of antioxidants, zinc, and potassium. To make them even more filling, dunk them in butter.

Cook Your Meat How You Like It

On the carnivore diet, you can prepare your meat however you want. The only exception is when a person decides to consume only raw meat.

Eating meat daily means you'll notice your tastes evolve over time, especially if you don't like your steak pink or slightly bloody. You'll probably start to prefer medium-rare steak over well-done steak.

Cooking should be preferred over raw in terms of food safety. Some raw meats are dangerous to consume, so cook them to ensure they are safe. However, raw seafood such as sushi, sashimi, salmon, tuna, or fresh oysters is a must-try.

Do Resistance Training Exercises

You can maintain or improve your lean body, particularly muscle mass, through resistance training. You must exercise regularly to start a carnivore diet to lose or keep your weight within a healthy range.

Resistance training includes lifting weights at home or the gym. Instead of lifting weights, you can do bodyweight exercises.

7-Day Carnivore Diet Food Plan

The carnivore diet is simple to begin. Here's an example of what a week on the carnivorous diet might look like.

Day	Breakfast	Lunch	Snack	Dinner
1	Eggs and Steak	Fried Pork and Salmon	Cheese and Cottage	Ground Beef Patties
2	Poached Eggs with Bacon	Tuna and Hard-Boiled Eggs	Sardines	Bone Broth and Roasted Chicken
3	Feta Cheese Omelet	Chicken Thighs with Cheddar Cheese	Chomps!	Ribeye Steak
4	Kefir and Two Eggs Over Medium	Shredded Chicken with Bacon	Tuna	Bison Burgers
5	Chicken and Feta Omelet	Beef Liver	Sardines	Pork Chops

| 6 | Chicken Livers and Scrambled Eggs | Turkey Burgers | Hard-Boiled Eggs | Slow-Roasted Salmon |
| 7 | Bacon and Eggs | Grilled Chicken Tenders | Steak Bites | Prime Rib |

Nothing needs to be overcomplicated. If you like steak, you can eat it for lunch, dinner, or even breakfast!

Surviving the First Month on the Carnivore Diet

Because the carnivore diet revolves around eating meat, it may appear simple to follow, but you may face a few unexpected challenges. As a result, in this section, we'll go over some things you can do to simplify your life, as well as some things to avoid.

Your focus, libido, appetite, and energy levels will fluctuate during the first week. The frequency with which you use the restroom will change. Sometimes for the better, sometimes for the worse.

Energy levels will begin to balance once your body becomes accustomed to ketosis. Although you may appear to have lost your appetite, you may experience mild hunger during the day.

You should be almost fully operational. There may be some residual effects from the adaptation phase. Although most of your adaptation is complete, it may take some time for your hormone, fluid, vitamin, and mineral levels to stabilize.

Here are some more tips and pointers to help you on your way to becoming a carnivore.

Get a Blood Test

Before beginning any diet, seeking medical or nutritional advice is critical. Have your blood tested before you begin and again two to three months later to assess the effects of your diet on your body.

You should also pay attention to things like digestion, weight, vitality, etc. Because everybody is unique and each person's response to the carnivore diet may differ from another's, it's important to monitor your body's progress before sticking with it for an extended time.

Expect Cravings

Being prepared for appetite, energy, and focus changes is a good idea. It's possible that some days you won't feel hungry at all, while others you'll crave a hearty lunch or even breakfast.

Make sure you have plenty of carnivore-friendly food available throughout the day because your appetite will fluctuate dramatically for the first few days, if not a week. Making microwaveable meals that satisfy your hunger is an excellent way to accomplish this.

Alternatively, you could stock up on cold-cut meats and eat them as a snack. You can make these ahead of time and then microwave them when you're hungry. If you do this, ensure they are entirely made of meat and not loaded with unnecessary ingredients.

Try Some Variety

Although eating steak every day may sound like a lot of fun, it's important to vary your meals while adhering to the diet's zero-carb and high-meat protein guidelines. On rare occasions, you may crave something sweet and high in carbohydrates instead of steak.

Ensure your meals vary by including cheese, salmon, and eggs to avoid this. If you have cravings and need a cheat day, eating something high in protein and satisfying your needs is best.

For example, peanut butter is an excellent way to maintain a high protein intake without consuming too many carbohydrates. It's preferable to reach for unhealthy snack items high in sugar, carbohydrates, and other harmful calories.

With these factors in mind, you should have no trouble surviving the first month of a carnivorous diet. Finally, you should pay close attention to what you eat and be prepared for changes in your energy and appetite. To reduce the likelihood of succumbing to cravings, try to empty your refrigerator before you begin. Keep track of your progress so you have something to compare it to in the future.

Chapter 2: Understanding the Science Behind the Carnivore Diet

Influential doctors like Robert Kiltz, Shawn Baker, and Paul Saladino have researched, supported, and promoted the health benefits of an all-meat diet.

Shawn Baker, a former orthopedic surgeon, pioneered the movement when he adopted an all-meat diet in 2016. In 2019, he wrote about his transition to carnivory, improved health, and the athletic success he attributes to this diet.

Dr. Paul Saladino, another movement pioneer, advocated "nose-to-tail" eating, which includes traditional cuts of meat, organ meats, and connective tissue. He also advocates for eating beef from grass-fed cows. Dr. Saladino is more than just a talented writer. He had severe eczema, an inflammatory skin condition that necessitated numerous intravenous steroids to control the inflammation, occasionally resulting in bleeding. Before learning about the carnivore diet, he unsuccessfully attempted some different diets, including plant-based and autoimmune protocols.

In 2020, podcast host Joe Rogan tried the regimen for one month, likely contributing to its popularity. He lived solely on eggs, elk, and grass-fed meat. He supplemented his micronutrient intake with fish oil and amino acids.

After 30 days, he noticed more energy and fewer daily aches. He was so pleased with the results that he went on to test slightly modified versions of the carnivorous diet.

The Evolutionary Perspective

Joe Rogan, the most-listened-to podcaster in the world, psychologist Jordan Peterson, and his daughter Mikhaila Peterson, a well-known health and wellness podcaster, are all proponents of the all-meat diet. Mikhaila developed an all-meat diet to treat various psychological and physical conditions, including rheumatoid arthritis, hypersomnia, Lyme disease, and eczema.

Jordan Peterson was also inspired to try the all-meat diet after seeing how well it worked for his daughter. Peterson stated in an interview with Joe Rogan that he lost 50 pounds. He also believed that his hunger had decreased by 70%. Blood sugar dysregulation does not bother him. He also mentioned that his anxiety and sadness had vanished, his mental clarity had improved, and his gum disease had disappeared.

The Evolutionary Basis

All proponents of meat diets argue that this radical departure from conventional nutritional wisdom is consistent with the evolution of human diets.

Scholars such as Miki Ben-Dor and Amber O'Hearn provide compelling evidence that our cavemen's forefathers lived on a carnivorous diet over roughly 2 million years of evolution.

Macronutrient and Micronutrient Considerations

Fatty beef is one of the foods with the highest nutrient density on the planet. In reality, a meat-only diet provides several vitalizing and necessary nutrients that are only found in meat, such as:

- D3
- B12
- Vitamin A (Retinol)
- Creatine
- Carnitine
- Carnosine
- Heme iron
- K2 (mk-4)
- Docosahexaenoic acid (DHA)
- Eicosapentaenoic Acid (EPA)
- Taurine

Let's examine some of these nutrients unique to meat in more detail.

Macronutrients On Carnivore

Getting your macros on a meat-based diet shouldn't be a problem if you're not afraid of fat. Choose 1-2 pounds of the beefed-up chops, and you've already met your daily requirement. Because it is so simple, you don't even need to monitor it. Protein is an excellent building block but a poor energy source, whereas fat is an excellent energy source. This applies to all diets; it's not just something to consider if you eat a lot of meat.

Carbohydrates, on the other hand, are unnecessary and will not count toward your needs. This is not to say they will not have a place. They are not required, but they may be beneficial in improving workout performance. And the truth is that most people do not practice them enough to be effective. You can get a reasonable amount of carbohydrates if you have compelling reasons to use dairy products, where the sugars are metabolized differently without causing many problems.

It's important to check your collagen consumption as a side issue from protein. Your body uses collagen, the predominant protein, to make bones and other non-muscle tissues. It's made from fish bones and bone broth. However, adding collagen powder, which can also be used to make protein shakes, is not harmful. As a result, the glycine (collagen) to methionine (muscle meat) ratio would be more evenly distributed, promoting tissue synthesis, sleep, and the release of soothing neurotransmitters.

Micronutrients On Carnivore

You should not be concerned about these nutrients in the carnivore diet. This category includes the micronutrients found in muscle meat; the primary food consumed by carnivores. Remember to eat 500-1000 grams of beef throughout the day.

How can you apply this knowledge to create a weekly grocery plan to allow your diet to last longer than the first few weeks? Based on the information above, you must only eat the foods listed below throughout the week to be healthy.

- Red Muscle Meat: Beef Steak, Ground Beef, 100% Beef Burgers – 7 days a week
- Energy Boosters: Butter, Beef Tallow – 3 plus days a week

- Multivitamins: Fish Roe, Eggs, Salmon, Beef Liver – 3 plus days a week
- Potential Supplements: Dextrose for workouts – 3 plus days a week
- Actual Supplements: Magnesium, Salt, Vitamin D, Iodine, Collagen – 7 days a week

The Impact of the Carnivore Diet on Health

According to proponents of the carnivore diet, residual pesticides and plant toxins used in producing plant foods are harmful to our health. They argue that the agricultural revolution was the first time starchy foods became a significant part of the human diet. Finally, it is suggested that the best way to avoid sugar for weight loss and metabolic health is to avoid all plant-based foods.

The authors of carnivore diet books frequently claim that decades of nutritional science research have resulted in incorrect dietary recommendations and present their topic as the solution to the world's obesity and noncommunicable chronic disease problems. According to most of these authors, since Homo sapiens evolved to hunt for meat and fish, eating plants was always a last resort during animal food scarcity.

What would happen if you ate only animal-derived foods for an extended period? Regrettably, there is no scientific evidence that removing all plant-based foods from the diet will harm health. Anecdotal reports and testimonies claim better weight management, improved heart and metabolic health, higher cognitive function, less inflammation, improved digestion, and remission of auto-immune diseases.

Nutrients in Meat Improve Digestion

Even a few weeks of vitamin A deficiency can alter the intestinal barrier-impairing microorganisms in your stomach.

Because vitamin D deficiency can weaken the barrier, it may be linked to inflammatory bowel disease and leaky gut.

Such deficiencies can be quickly remedied by consuming an all-meat diet high in fat-soluble vitamins from fatty cuts of steak and organ meats.

Furthermore, certain meat-derived amino acids may be beneficial to gut health. Glutamate-rich foods, such as beef and eggs, help to control tight joints and reduce permeability to toxins.

Carnivore Diets Cut Carbs

According to conventional nutritional guidelines, we should eat three meals and two snacks daily, all high-carb fruits and vegetables.

The all-meat diet sees this advice, as well as the SAD's excessive carbohydrate intake, as the primary causes of the following civilizational diseases, among others:

- Heart Disease
- Hypertension
- Type 2 Diabetes
- Epithelial Cell Cancers
- Inflammatory

Debunking Common Myths about the Carnivore Diet

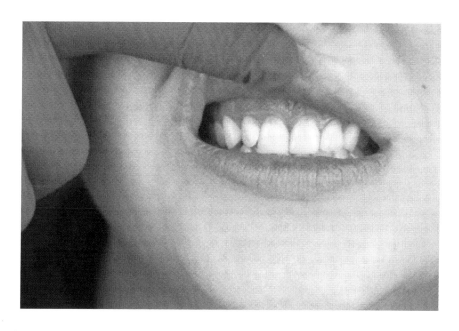

Causes Colon Cancer

Numerous claim eating meat causes cancer. On the other hand, the allegation is yet another example of explicit inferences drawn from flimsy relationships. There is a reason why epidemiological studies are regarded as poor science; there are simply too many variables involved to convert correlating lines into solid evidence, of which there are none.

Meanwhile, a rat study shows that bacon has a preventative effect on malignant growth. Another study claims that red meat can be used to treat pre-existing tumors. Nothing in the world should cause you to be concerned about the impact of a carnivore's diet on your colon.

Causes Scurvy

Vitamin C deficiency is the most common and visible vitamin deficiency in carnivores. Scurvy is caused directly by a lack of this vitamin. The most obvious sign is death, but you may also experience less serious symptoms such as swollen gums and easy bruising.

Although vitamin C has other advantages, its primary function is to prevent scurvy. It is frequently stated that eating meat does not provide this vitamin. However, this is incorrect. This vitamin is present in 2.5mg per 100 grams of fresh beef. That may not be enough to meet your 40mg requirement. The 25mg of beef should meet your body's requirements when combined with your steak total.

You Need Fiber to Pass out Feces

Fiber increases stool size, but this does not necessarily imply that bowel movements are more efficient. Fiber, in reality, is a very ineffective food source. Fiber can only meet 4% of our energy requirements.

This is the wrong way to treat a sore stomach; instead, it will aggravate the situation. As they move through the system, undigested fiber fragments are passed to the stomach and intestines. At the very least, there is a compelling case for a leaky gut.

Meanwhile, a carnivorous diet should result in small, frequent bowel movements. Allow for a period of adjustment at least once.

Causes Your Kidneys Harm

In addition to its association with MTOR (Protein that regulates many cell functions), a high protein count is linked to decreased kidney function, including kidney stones. A large part of this link can be attributed to protein leakage in the urine, one of the first symptoms of damaged kidneys.

This is a well-known myth that has been spreading for years, fueling concern about the effects of a high-protein diet. However, despite the possibility of a mechanism, no evidence of the crime appears to exist.

Although pre-existing conditions can make it more difficult to filter amino acids effectively, this is an exception.

Thus, eating a lot of protein does not increase your risk of organ failure. Once again, the body can handle massive amounts of an evolved food source.

Causes Global Warming

Livestock has been frequently cited as one of the primary causes of climate change, which is true. They waste valuable land that could be used for profitable and sustainable crops, contribute to droughts, and emit hazardous gases into the atmosphere.

What would happen if the cow was removed from the scenario? Regardless, rain falls on the ground. We're not talking about rerouting water or extracting it from wells. Agriculture uses 70% of the world's fresh and groundwater, so that's taken care of.

The FAO claims the global cattle industry produces more greenhouse gases than the entire transportation industry. The main culprit is methane, which is produced by cattle. Methane has a short life cycle and degrades after ten years, which the carbon equation does not account for.

Cattle's ability to store carbon in the soil is also overlooked. When raised on regenerating pastures, they have a net negative impact on carbon emissions.

To make matters worse, the FAO data included the entire beef production chain, excluding the transit phase. Transportation and livestock produce 5% and 14% of direct emissions.

The idea that converting grazing lands to grow more vegetables would be best for the planet is counterproductive. Currently, 70% of agricultural land is better suited to cattle and wild animals than crop production. The landscape simply does not support a plant-centered vision.

In other words, the allegations leveled against livestock are simply false. Ruminants, in particular, have played an important role in the environment for our survival as a species. The notion that they could be the ones destroying everything is ridiculous. However, the proposed alternatives have only existed since the agricultural revolution or for less than 10,000 years.

No Phytochemicals

Dietitians advise consuming a variety of foods for good reasons. Non-nutritive substances known as phytochemicals are said to have positive health effects. Some well-known examples are isoflavones, isothiocyanates, curcumin, and resveratrol. Longevity, hormone support, and decreased inflammation are a few advantages of these nutrients. The caveat is in the name itself:

phytochemicals are unique to plants. Hence, a carnivorous diet excludes you from a variety of wonder substances.

Although phytochemicals may have medical applications, they shouldn't be considered a cure-all. There is undoubtedly proof of negative side effects in people.

Isoflavones, included in soy products, are phytoestrogens, which bind to estrogen receptors and produce a lesser form of estrogen. It is a hormone disruptor that the plant has developed expressly to stop predators from reproducing. Even resveratrol, a revered vitamin for fending off the fires of aging, can sometimes enhance oxidative damage because it is a phytoestrogen and shares the same potential to mess with your hormones.

And to cap it all, many of these purportedly plant-only compounds can be found in grass-fed meat and milk, like phenols, terpenoids, carotenoids, and antioxidants. Ruminants' ability to digest plant stuff and provide us with bioavailable plant nutrients is their specialty.

Throughout millions of years, which comprised most of our species' existence, carnivore was likely the predominant food of our paleolithic ancestors. The current notion that meat is unhealthy does not fit with this reality at all. Because people started eating more plants 10,000 years ago, specialized biological adaptations didn't disappear.

We eat meat, and we still do, and the carnivorous diet is arguably the most secure. No evidence exists that a carnivorous diet harms health until that situation changes.

Chapter 3: Creating a Healthy and Sustainable Carnivore Lifestyle

There are valid reasons why some people prefer to avoid plant foods in favor of a meat-based diet, also known as the Carnivore Diet. Who, and why, would choose such a radical way of life? Is it advantageous?

Sustainability Considerations

Being vegan may make ethical sense, but the health benefits aren't compelling. The carnivorous diet, on the other hand, is a different story. As a result, we only need to address the issue of sustainability.

Even when compared to a vegan's grocery list, the options for carnivores are quite limited. Most people on carnivore aren't going out into the woods to hunt elk, but there's always the possibility that you have access to a few extra species of wild game.

Pursuing adequate nutrition is at the forefront of the fight against inflammation, illness, poor mental health, obesity, and performance.

Although a plant-based diet may be the most environmentally friendly option, it is not always the most practical or readily available option for everyone. There are environmentally friendly ways to consume meat and dairy products. Being more selective about where you get your meat can make a huge difference. Reduced consumption of less sustainable products will also have a greater impact than expected.

How to Choose Sustainable Meat Sources

When you do eat meat, consider which options are the most environmentally friendly:

- Purchase meat from local farmers or ranches where the livestock is fed grass.
- Choose pasture-raised meat; it is the most environmentally friendly option because it mimics a more "natural" form. Pasture-bred animals can forage naturally, reducing their reliance on agriculture and the grains that would otherwise be required. These animals are free to eat plants, are not restrained, and can behave naturally.

Pasture-raised animals are the best option for ecology and animal welfare, so spend your money wisely and make a sustainable choice! Fish, chicken, and pork are better choices for the environment. Seafood, such as mussels, oysters, and scallops, has a lower carbon footprint. Examine companies and supermarkets that strive to source their meat, dairy, and seafood from sustainable sources.

Choosing the Right Meats and Animal Products

What Can You Eat on the Carnivore Diet?

Those looking for an alternative to the typical ketogenic diet to reduce inflammation caused by meals, avoid food groups that cause digestion issues, or find a more satisfying way to lose weight increasingly turn to the Carnivore Diet. Although the "Carnivore Diet" clearly states that meat is the main component of the diet, there are some nuances to consider before beginning. We'll review your options for cooking delicious meals while on a carnivore diet in greater detail.

Golden Rule of the Carnivore Diet

The cardinal rule of the carnivore diet is to eat only meat. Isn't that a fantastic diet? You can make the meat-only diet work for you by selecting and properly preparing the right types of meat. Eating nothing but bacon all day will not get you the desired results, but eating only chicken breast will quickly become monotonous.

Carnivore Diet Food List: What to Eat and What Not to Eat On the Carnivore Diet

It appears simple enough to eat meat until you begin to crave pizza, waffles, or tacos. At that point, you realize how limiting a carnivore diet can be. Even seemingly simple tasks, such as finding the perfect flavors, can be difficult. We'll show you how to make wise choices so you can prepare satisfying meals with few ingredients.

Making Good Meat Choices

The carnivore diet emphasizes meats high in animal fat, protein, and other essential nutrients. We know that different cuts of meat contain different amounts of fat and different nutrients, vitamins, and minerals. You should limit your carbohydrate intake as much as possible because the carnivore diet encourages your body to burn fat rather than carbohydrates.

Seafood

A well-balanced seafood diet includes one of the wisest foods available: flesh. Furthermore, it does not always have to be lake trout. You can add scallops, shrimp, clams, and other shellfish to the interesting varieties of fish you'll find in the freezer section. Salmon has some of the highest levels of Omega-3 fatty acids in fish, and swai, a type of Southeast Asian catfish that cooks up clean and slightly sweet, are both excellent options.

Organ Meats

Beef liver is one of those foods that aren't on everyone's list of favorite foods. Beef liver should be one of the animal products you include in your carnivore diet plan because the flavor is achieved through proper cooking. The liver is one of the best ways to ensure you get enough vitamin C on a carnivore diet. It is a nutrient-dense animal protein with numerous applications. Cow liver pancakes have also been seen elsewhere.

Pork Skin

Pork skin is one of the easiest animal products to incorporate into a carnivore keto diet. When fried, it is known as pork rind or chicharrones. In either case, properly cooked skin and fat become light and airy while retaining flavorful beneficial fats. A carnivore diet does not technically have a food pyramid because it consists entirely of animal products, but if it did, pork rinds would be one of the larger portions.

Eggs

It is critical to include eggs in your diet. While making your shopping list for the carnivorous diet, buy five dozen eggs at a time. You should keep hard-boiled eggs on hand at all times for snacks, as well as for lunch and dinner. Eggs are a nutrient-dense, high-protein food that promotes intestinal health.

Meats to Avoid

Certain meats on the carnivore diet meal plan should be avoided. Many processed meat portions, in particular, are unhealthy and may contain excessive foods not recommended for carnivores.

Avoid including pepperoni and other processed meat snacks on your carnivore diet meal plan. Dairy products can contain more carbs, and wide bacon varieties contain a lot of preservatives and other chemicals. Finding low-lactose dairy products and incorporating them into your carnivore diet meal plan can help you lose body fat while controlling your blood sugar levels.

Most Nutrient Dense Carnivore Foods

The carnivore diet includes nutrient-dense meats that are frequently high in saturated fat. Bone broth and bone marrow, which have high nutritional value, can be added to low-fat foods like chicken. Bone broth is also an excellent post-workout snack for those seeking muscle gain.

Beef liver is the healthiest food to include in your diet to ensure adequate nutrient intake. Beef liver has numerous benefits for carnivores, including being a superior source of vitamin C and other essential nutrients. Add beef liver to ground beef patties if you find cow liver unappealing.

The Best Ways to Source Carnivore Foods

Even though the carnivore diet emphasizes eating a lot of meat, getting the best meat possible is critical when adhering to such a strict diet. Eating the healthiest meat can lower your risk of colon cancer and renal failure while maintaining regular bowel movements. When possible, the best way to source beef is to go large. Many people will discover that they can buy quarter or half-cuts of animals for a few dollars per pound, allowing them to design the best all-meat diets by selecting the preferred cuts.

If you can't go directly to the source, you should try to get animal items with clear labeling to determine whether the meat is grass-fed, antibiotic-free, and correctly harvested. Grass-fed meat is thought to be more nutrient-dense than grain-fed meat, making it a better option for an elimination diet.

The nutritional value of high-lactose dairy products varies as well. Goat milk may be preferable to cow milk for some carnivorous diets. Sticking to a low-carb diet will be more difficult if you plan to consume milk, butter, and other dairy products.

Supplements and Nutritional Considerations

The carnivore diet is the pinnacle of elimination dieting; it requires you to eat only foods derived naturally from animals and to avoid anything that causes discomfort or swelling in your gut.

Because of the diet's stringent requirements, cheap sports supplements with garishly colored labels and processed ingredients are prohibited.

Unfortunately, our food is not as nutrient-dense as our forefathers due to modern agriculture, so even a perfect carnivore diet requires some supplementation to achieve optimum health. We recommend a few supplements due to the negative effects of switching to a carnivorous diet after years of eating grains and vegetables.

These are some of our favorite natural carnivore diet supplements. It should be noted that no supplement can replace real food, but if you're just starting, these will simplify your diet and help you achieve better results.

Beef Organs — The Ultimate Multivitamin

To fully benefit from the carnivore way of life, you should eat from head to tail. Consuming the entire animal, including its organs, is required. Because most people dislike cooking or preparing offal, it can be taken in pill form.

Organ meat supplements are made by companies such as Ancestral Supplements and Heart & Soil Supplements, and they only contain desiccated (dried) meat from grass-fed cattle, which retains all the nutrients found in fresh organs.

We recommend beginning with Ancestral Supplements and Beef Organs. It contains the ideal carnivore multivitamin and a liver, heart, kidney, spleen, and pancreas.

Electrolytes — No More Carnivore Side Effects

Once you eat meat exclusively, you may experience carnivore diet side effects such as headache, diarrhea, and even heart palpitations. Both of these are frequently caused by dehydration and electrolyte deficiency.

Interact. This causes your body to lose sodium and alters your electrolyte balance, resulting in "keto flu."

Consuming electrolytes, in other words, will make the transition to a carnivorous diet much easier. We also recommend them for carnivore dieters who exercise vigorously.

Ox Bile — Digest Fat Easier

A high-fat carnivore diet takes some time to adjust to. Many people who are used to a high-carbohydrate diet experience bloating and digestive problems when they switch to a meat-only diet.

To help with this, you must strengthen your gallbladder and produce more bile to digest all that fat.

Anyone experiencing digestive issues or following a carnivorous diet without a gallbladder should take ox bile as a supplement.

Vitamin C — Difficult to Get from Just Meat

When you first started eating only meat, you were probably asked, "Aren't you going to get scurvy?"

Of course, they have no idea what they're talking about, and a carnivorous diet is perfectly safe. However, organ meats such as beef liver provide most of the vitamin C in this diet. As a result, if you eat mostly steaks and muscle meat, you may not be getting enough vitamin C. (or less nutritious, less expensive grain-fed meat).

One approach is to take a vitamin C supplement. Once your body has experienced the healing benefits of the carnivore diet, another is to switch to a carnivore diet with fruit or an ancestral diet.

Collagen — Heal Your Gut

Although your body produces less collagen as you age and studies have shown its benefits for your appearance, most people consider collagen a skin supplement.

Collagen is good for your gut microbiome and can help heal the "leaky gut," so it makes our list. This disorder causes an immune response and inflammation because your gut allows more particles than usual to enter your bloodstream, including toxins and undigested food.

The carnivore diet is beneficial for inflammation because it excludes foods that irritate your gut, allowing it to heal. Collagen supplements can help to speed up this process. Consider it a long-term strategy; by repairing your gut sooner rather than later, you'll reap the benefits of a carnivorous diet and absorb more nutrients from your meals sooner.

Stearic Acid — Get Your Body to Shape

The final item on the list may appear strange, but it could be the perfect supplement if you follow the carnivore diet to lose weight or improve your body composition. When people discover they aren't losing weight, they may not be eating enough fat or following the incorrect carnivore diet macros.

It has been shown that the long-chain fatty acid, stearic acid, found in animal fats, can help with belly fat reduction. The best sources are fatty meat cuts and dishes made with animal fat rather than oil.

To boost your energy and experience the fat-burning benefits, we recommend a supplement containing beef suet, such as Heart & Soil's Fire starter.

Alternatives to Carnivore Supplements

Even though the supplements on this list are safe and effective, you may want to eat more of a specific food to achieve the same results.

Sea Salt

An excellent replacement for electrolytes and ideal for replenishing sodium levels. Redmond Sea Salt is an excellent choice for a carnivorous diet.

Beef Liver Crisps

A healthy alternative to eating fresh or raw cow liver or taking a beef liver supplement. Many companies make beef liver crisps, similar to beef jerky but healthier. The taste of liver is still present, albeit more subdued.

Bone Broth

Although we recommend making your bone broth for the carnivore diet, several companies sell ready-made bone broth if you don't want to cook or keep all the ingredients on hand.

Beef Tallow and Suet

However, if you want to reap the benefits of stearic acid without cooking with healthy animal fat, you can simply add some tallow or suet to your diet.

What Supplements Would You Need to Take?

You might wonder what supplements you'd need to take if you tried the carnivore diet. You should take several supplements to ensure you get all your daily nutrients.

1. **Vitamin D** — This is one of the most important vitamins to consume if you follow a carnivorous diet. This is because vitamin D is not widely distributed in the diet. Vitamin D is found in small amounts in foods such as fish, eggs, and cheese, but it is insufficient to keep your body functioning properly. You should take a vitamin D supplement to ensure adequate vitamin D levels.
2. **Vitamin K2** — Vitamin K2 is another dietary supplement you should take if you're on the carnivore diet or any other high-fat diet. This is because vitamin K2 aids calcium absorption in the body. You risk developing osteoporosis if you do not consume vitamin K2.
3. **Multivitamin** — If you follow a carnivore diet, you should also take this supplement. This supplement will help you get enough of all the other vitamins and minerals you would normally get from fruits and vegetables.

4. **Fiber** — If you're following the carnivore diet, you must also consume some fiber. This is because most carnivorous dieters do not consume any vegetables, which are high in fiber.
5. **Creatine** — If you regularly exercise while on the carnivore diet, you may want to take creatine. This is done so you can reap additional benefits from your workouts due to creatine.
6. **Collagen** — Collagen supplements are also recommended when following a carnivorous diet. This is because it may help to repair any damage to your connective tissues and joints.

The Role of Exercise in the Carnivore Lifestyle

Exercising on the carnivore diet is similar to exercising on any other type of diet, but there are a few things to keep in mind if you want to improve your results. Some workout approaches, for example, may be more difficult depending on how "fat-oriented" you are at various points in your carnivorous journey.

Are workouts necessary?

No. The carnivore diet does not necessitate physical activity. However, there is a significant reason why it is so beneficial.

People follow the carnivore diet for various reasons, including autoimmune disorders, weight loss, and overall health. Most of these are affected by the amount and sensitivity of your insulin.

The more insulin resistant you are, the more difficult it will be to lose weight, get healthy, and manage your autoimmune sensitivity.

Exercise is one of the best ways to increase insulin sensitivity because the muscles are the primary sites of insulin uptake. In other words, larger, more toned muscles help regulate insulin.

Bodybuilding On the Carnivore Diet

One of the most difficult topics for people following a carnivorous diet is whether or not you need carbs to gain muscle. Carbohydrates aren't required to build muscle, but they do help because you need three things in your diet:

- **Testosterone** – Because testosterone is derived from cholesterol, it is unsurprising that some people experience an increase in testosterone when they switch to a carnivorous diet. Be at ease, ladies. Because testosterone is used to produce estrogen, a carnivore will not turn you into a man.
- **Insulin-Like Growth Factor (IGF-1)** – A carnivorous diet is not advised. IGF-1 is produced using insulin. If you have low insulin levels due to eating a few dietary carbs, your IGF-1 levels will be low.
- **Growth Hormone (GH)** – Although the body produces growth hormone naturally, there are ways to increase it, such as fasting and exercise.

If you want to gain muscle on a carnivorous diet, you should probably supplement with carbs, keeping the muscle-building recipe in mind.

Strength Training On the Carnivore Diet

Because so little reliable research is available, much conflicting information exists on strength training when following a carnivorous diet. One of the most common myths about strength training is that you need a lot of carbs to lift a heavyweight.

When considering a strength-to-weight ratio, most experienced low-carb strong men always return to or surpass their prior personal bests, even though this may be true during the fat-adaptation phase.

In other words, strength athletes will likely become smaller due to decreased fat mass and lack of water retention, but their muscle mass will increase due to increased protein intake.

As a result, building strength necessitates intense, physiologically demanding training that may necessitate carbohydrate supplementation.

Endurance Training On the Carnivore Diet

Because it requires the fewest short bursts of energy and burns much fat as fuel, the carnivore diet is likely to perform best during endurance exercise. Many endurance athletes now use low- or no-carb diets to fuel their workouts and competitions.

Sport-Specific Training On the Carnivore Diet

Whether eating carnivorous while competing in sports is a good idea is still unclear. The carnivore diet can help you become stronger, faster, and fitter, but incorporating it into your training and competition schedule can be difficult.

It makes no sense, for example, to try to become fat-adapted just a few weeks before a major event. Consuming carbohydrates during certain events may be acceptable even if you are fat-adapted.

Chapter 4: Carnivore Meal Planning and Preparation

To get going with the carnivore diet, you must have a diet plan and follow it.

How to Prepare a Carnivore Diet Meal Plan

The following suggestions can help you stay motivated and well-prepared for a full carnivore diet meal.

Plan to Give all Your Commitment

Following a high-carnivore diet over a few days or weeks requires complete focus and commitment. The worst thing you can do is follow the carnivore diet day by day, waiting until the morning to decide what to eat next. Set weekly goals instead and plan your meals with a carnivore diet food list and a diet planner.

You can also devote more time to researching meat sources and cooking techniques to diversify your diet.

You can even try eating animal parts like the liver and heart to try different nutrition options and taste new sensations.

While on a carnivore diet, you can use delivery services if you don't want to prepare meals.

Know the Reason for Deciding on the Carnivore Diet

Setting goals is essential before embarking on the carnivore diet. Remember this is a lifestyle change; you must consume only animal products and plenty of healthy fat.

You must understand why you embark on the carnivore diet, whether to lose weight, reduce body fat, manage food sensitivities, reverse an autoimmune condition, or gain lean muscle. Based on your requirements, you must establish a clear objective.

Whether your goal is to gain six pounds of lean muscle in seven months or to lose ten pounds before the end of the year, you must strictly adhere to the meat-only diet plan throughout the entire process.

Be Socially Prepared

Eating in public is one of the most feared situations when following a carnivorous diet.

People won't judge you if you eat as they do at a party. When you reveal that you follow a carnivore diet, which includes consuming primarily red meat, animal fat, and no plant items, the entire table will attack you.

Inform them that you are attempting a carnivorous diet to identify the root causes of your numerous food allergy concerns or that you are attempting to overcome some health conditions. People will still try to convince you that your decision is wrong. Never let any of their opinions demotivate you. Regardless of what others say, keep working and focus on your goal.

In this situation, asking if they are more concerned about their health or yours is the best action. They should come to respect you for what you are attempting to accomplish by adopting this eating pattern.

After you've finished preparing, look at four different carnivore diets and review a weekly grocery list and meal plan for each.

Meal Planning 101

Meal plans for carnivore diets are classified into four categories based on how restrictive they are and whether or not they include organ meats.

Standard Meal Plan

The typical or standard carnivore meal plan's main components are ruminant meats and good fats. Pork, poultry, fish, and shellfish round out the menu with various nutrients and flavors.

The carnivore diet is often used to treat digestive issues. Because of this, avoiding potentially irritating dairy products for the first 4-6 weeks is recommended.

Nose-to-Tail with Dairy Meal Plan

Nose-to-tail feeding is the closest thing to how our forefathers ate for most of history. This food group comprises organ meats and unusual animal parts such as liver and bone marrow.

Eating an animal from head to tail entails consuming and savoring every part of it rather than just the desirable parts. This means you eat tasty organs, fat, and unpopular body parts.

The nose-to-tail diet prioritizes organ meats high in healthy fat and nutrients over all other types of meat. Our forefathers ate this way, and hunter-gatherer tribes continue to do so today. Some of them even throw what we would consider meat to the dogs!

The Lion Diet Meal Plan

Even though the lion diet is extremely simple, it is critical to remember to select the fattiest portions of meat. It's an elimination diet that helps with gut healing. The average American diet frequently harms the nervous system and gastrointestinal tract. The lion diet helps to alleviate this. Only salt, water, and meat from ruminant animals are permitted on the Lion's Diet.

Consider the Lion diet an elimination procedure that can help you restore the balance of your gut flora and other metabolic parameters that the Standard American Diet has disrupted.

Because your body will release glycogen during this time, monitoring your body while on the lion's diet is critical. Make sure you get enough salt and water.

Other animal products, such as eggs and organ meats, will eventually be added back to help you meet your nutritional needs.

Carnivore Adjacent Meal Plan

A "carnivore adjacent" diet includes 80-90 percent whole food animal products, with the remaining 10-20% coming from low-toxicity, low-carb fruits, and vegetables.

Even if Lion's diet does not offer the same weight-loss benefits, it does provide a more sustainable way of eating that can appeal to our need for variety. It also allows for additional modifications to meet the demands and goals of each individual's health.

Grocery Shopping for the Carnivore Diet

If you follow a carnivore diet that only consists of animal products, a surprising number of foods can be included on your grocery list for shopping.

This list of foods for a carnivore diet is provided to help you create the most nutrient-dense diet possible to meet your specific health goals.

Beef

- Ribeye steak
- T-bone steak
- Ground beef
- Brisket
- Short ribs or back ribs

- Skirt Steak
- Tri-tip steak
- Chuck Roast
- Tenderloin
- Porterhouse Steak
- Strip loin

Seafood & Lamb

- Shrimp/lobster
- Salmon, mackerel
- Oysters
- Scallops
- Muscles
- Ground lamb
- Lamb shanks
- Crabs
- Lamb chops
- Clams

Chicken & Pork

- Rotisserie chicken
- Chicken wings
- Chicken
- Rotisserie chicken
- Chicken drumsticks
- Chicken breast
- Chicken thighs
- Pork ribs

- Chicken wings
- Pork belly
- Bacon
- Pork chops
- Pork shoulder
- Pork butt

Organ Meats

- Liver
- Heart
- Oxtail
- Cheeks
- Tongue
- Brain
- Kidneys
- Feet

Less Optimal Foods

- Cheese
- Eggs
- Bacon
- Cured meats
- Heavy cream
- Yogurt
- Milk
- Sausage

Simple and Delicious Carnivore Recipes

What should you eat if you're a carnivore? Meat-based ingredients such as beef, pig, eggs, fish, salt, and dairy are used in these Carnivore Diet dishes. Certain dishes may contain trace amounts of spices or plant-based flavors, depending on how tasty you want your diet to be.

1. *Easy Cheeseburger Pie*

This simple cheeseburger pie is perfect for a relaxing dinner any day of the week! Because it is flavored with simple, everyday ingredients, it will surely become a new family favorite. Furthermore, these low-cost ingredients are usually already in your refrigerator.

Total Time Required: 30 minutes

Servings: 6

Ingredients:

- 1½ lb. ground beef
- 1 medium onion diced
- 1 tbsp. tallow/cooking fat of choice
- 4 whole eggs
- ½ tsp. garlic powder
- ½ tsp. ground mustard
- ½ tsp. salt
- ½ tsp. ground black pepper
- 1 c. shredded cheese

Instructions:

1. Preheat the oven to 350°F and grease a 9-inch circular pie plate. Brown the meat in cooking grease in a heavy-bottomed skillet or frying pan. Transfer to a pie dish once finished.
2. Brown the onions in a little extra fat in the skillet for about seven minutes. Make sure to stir frequently.
3. While the onions are cooking, whisk the eggs. Season with salt and pepper. Pour over the beef and allow to soak. Shake the dish gently if necessary.
4. Distribute the onions evenly over the eggs and sausage. Sprinkle cheese over the entire pie.
5. To melt and bubble the cheese, bake for 20 minutes. Allow the cheeseburger pie to rest for about five minutes before cutting.

6. For a complete hamburger-themed supper, serve on a bed of lettuce with a side of pickles or pickle relish and thick slices of fresh tomatoes. Place sugar-free ketchup and mustard on the table.

2. Carnivore Meatballs with Beef Heart

This recipe can easily be doubled; simply use a larger pan and remember that cooking will take longer. Carnivore-style meatballs are simple to make (three ingredients and four simple steps) and high in CoQ10, selenium, zinc, and other essential nutrients.

Total Time Required: 25 minutes

Servings: 4

Material: 8×8-inch square size glass baking dish

Ingredients:

- 1 tsp. salt
- 8 oz. ground beef
- 8 oz. ground beef heart

Instructions:

1. In a bowl, thoroughly combine the two ground meat portions. Season with salt.
2. Scoop about 2 ounces and roll it into a ball between your palms.

3. Place the finished product in a small glass baking dish.
4. Bake for 20 minutes at 350°F in a preheated oven.
5. The juices drip onto the baking dish when the meat is fully cooked. Warm the meatballs and serve with the sauce on the side.

3. Tartare

Tartare, or steak tartare, is raw or nearly raw beef garnished with egg yolk. Tartare can also be made with raw or nearly raw tuna. It can also be made with beef or red meats such as bison, lamb, or elk!

Ingredients:

- 1 tsp. apple cider or balsamic vinegar
- 12 oz. lean beef
- 2 tsp. brown or Dijon mustard
- 2 egg yolks (optional)
- 1 tsp. salt

Instructions:

1. If you want to dice the meat very small, freeze it for about 20 minutes. Remove it from the freezer, cut it into thin strips, and divide it into tiny cubes.

2. In a mixing bowl, combine and thoroughly mix all of the ingredients.
3. Serve the tartare. To serve, dip in the tartare mound's top and gently place the egg yolk on top. Eat as soon as possible because the marinade turns the meat mushy, and the leftovers don't keep well.

Instead of just beef, experiment with other red meats such as lamb, bison, or even elk.

4. Egg Pudding

Egg pudding is made with three animal-based ingredients and is ready in 5 minutes. Try this carnivore diet dessert for a sweet treat with no fiber.

Total Time Required: 2 hours 5 minutes

Servings: 2

Ingredients:

- 4 oz. half & half
- 5 soft-boiled eggs peeled
- 2 ½ tbsp. sweetener
- 1 pinch salt
- 1 tbsp. softened grass-fed butter,
- 1 tsp. vanilla extract

Instructions:

1. In a blender, combine all of the ingredients and blend until smooth. As needed, taste and adjust the sweetener.
2. Chill in the refrigerator for 2 hours before serving.

Notes:

Consider your priorities and goals; make the best decision for you.

- If you're a strict carnivore, remove the sweetener and vanilla extract.
- If you're increasing carbohydrates, use raw honey instead of sweetener.
- If you're a keto carnivore, use a low-carb sweetener. To begin, 2 ½ tablespoons of sweetener are recommended. You could increase the amount to 4 tablespoons.

Eating Out and Traveling on the Carnivore Diet

The good news for those on a carnivore diet is that numerous restaurants will accommodate your needs with high-quality, healthy meats. Your best bet is to eat at steakhouses and barbecue joints.

However, avoid processed animal foods. The carnivore diet for weight loss prohibits the consumption of processed foods. Simply pay attention to how the food is prepared. When following a carnivore diet, avoiding foods stir-fried with vegetables or containing sauces is critical.

Simply pay attention to how the food is prepared. Unfortunately, because almost all Chinese, American, and Indian cuisines rely heavily on salt, carbohydrates, and sauces, you should probably avoid eating there if you're a carnivore.

Navigating the American Food Landscape on the Carnivore Diet

Many Americans struggle to transition from an American food landscape to a carnivore diet because most foods are high in carbohydrates.

The good news is that you can easily transition from these high-carb diets to carnivorous diets by using simple strategies. The typical American diet, whether you follow the food pyramid or eat too much junk food:

- Diets that include fruit, honey, and sweet potatoes are said to be paleo.
- Dairy-free diet
- Gluten-free diet
- Vegan and vegetarian diets

Any other eating plan that includes grains, fruit, sugar, or a natural sweetener at least once a day is typical of Americans.

Carbohydrate-based diets are common in developed countries such as the United States. This implies that they primarily rely on glucose, which they obtain from carbohydrates, to fuel their bodies and brains.

Following one of these diets will make transitioning to a carnivore easier.

If you are a "carb burner" who consumes more than 30 grams of carbohydrates per day, you have two options for starting the carnivore diet:

1. To get fat-adapted, 4-6 weeks on the ketogenic (keto) diet is a good place to start before beginning the carnivore diet.
2. Begin the carnivore diet as soon as possible. Although challenging for the first six weeks, you will grow accustomed to it.

If you want to start eating meat immediately, follow the Carnivore Meal Plan's instructions for eating only animal products and no plants for the next six weeks while your body adjusts.

If you decide to begin the keto diet first, familiarize yourself with it and allow yourself one month of meat-heavy keto to allow your body to adjust to ketosis.

When people switch from the keto to the carnivore diet, their bodies are already in ketosis and fat-adapted. Being fat-adapted makes the transition to carnivore much easier.

Fat adaptation is the process of adapting to use ketones as fuel. Fat adaptation manifests as:

- Ketone strips detect fewer ketones in your urine.
- Having more endurance when exercising.
- The ability to go for extended periods without feeling hungry or dizzy.

Because you are already accustomed to being in ketosis and because keto has probably already reduced inflammation and slowed your cravings for carbohydrates, transitioning to a carnivorous diet is relatively easy and simple.

Substituting Popular American Foods with Carnivore-Friendly Alternatives

The most popular American foods can be found in various restaurants, ranging from upscale to casual, in backyards for large or intimate gatherings, and everywhere. They will make your mouth water.

Maintaining your health and financial goals may be difficult. This section compiles a list of helpful substitutes to make this year's transition to a carnivorous diet easier for you.

Standard hot dogs should be replaced with turkey or chicken sausage. Although hotdogs are a popular and tasty party food, meat products, particularly red and processed meats like hot dogs, contain a lot of saturated fat. According to our data, they contain an average of 21% of the DV for saturated fat per serving, compared to roughly 25% for processed lunch meats.

Replace Burgers with Carnivore Burgers

A carnivore burger will almost certainly be a mainstay during meal preparation if you follow an extremely low-carb animal-based diet.

A no-carb burger bun only requires two ingredients.

You can use this as carnivorous sandwich bread, load it with your favorite animal-based sandwich toppings, and make grilled cheese and hamburgers with ground beef or hamburger meat.

So far, this is a fantastic bread alternative for carnivore diets. After you've prepared the buns, you can stuff them with your favorite carnivore burger toppings. Take a look at the list of topping and filling ideas below. Here's what is needed to make the buns:

- Cheese
- Eggs

Replace French Fries with Carnivore French Fries

In addition to being simple to prepare, keto French fries made with almond flour taste the most like the fast food fries we crave. When it's burger night, your family will appreciate these low-carb French fries' appearance, texture, and flavor. You'll also appreciate the fact that these keto fries can be frozen.

Replace Pizza with Carnivore Pizza

In Greece, a carnivore diet or carnivore pizza would be absolute bliss! You could live as a gourmet carnivore in any Mediterranean country. This area may also have the healthiest sources of lamb, wild game, goat, snails, shellfish, and eggs. The list dates back to ancient times when a 24-hour-baked cow stuffed with a lamb and a small wild boar was a popular holiday dish. In addition, the piglet was stuffed with a turkey, then a duck, and finished with quails filled with seafood or eggs.

Replace Ice Cream with Dairy Desserts

A summer picnic would be incomplete without some delectable sweets. And what better way to unwind than with ice cream?

The carnivore diet aims to eat more like our hunter-gatherer forefathers rather than the modern eating habits slowly killing us. The Carnivore Diet is built around a simple equation.

The Carnivore Diet meal plan can help you achieve your goals safely and sustainably. Whether you want to improve your health by avoiding processed foods or reach your fitness goals by increasing your protein intake, simply follow the guidelines, and you'll be there in no time.

Chapter 5: Carnivore Cuisine for Breakfast

Because breakfast is considered the day's most important meal, we've compiled a list of the best, healthiest carnivore diet breakfast options to keep you satisfied and on track.

Classic Carnivore Breakfasts

1. Bacon and Eggs

A popular and well-liked continental breakfast that is incredibly satisfying and tasty is bacon and eggs. It is one of the finest Keto breakfasts.

Serving Size: 4

Ingredients:

- 8 egg
- Salt as needed
- ½ c. cherry tomatoes
- ¼ c. parsley
- 150 g. bacon
- Black pepper, as required

Instructions:

1. Cook the bacon in a skillet. Cook until crispy in a skillet over medium-low heat.
2. Cook the eggs and cherry tomatoes in a skillet. Eggs can be cooked in the same pan as the potatoes. Cover the pan to ensure thorough egg cooking. Cherry tomatoes are cut into slices and cooked in the pan simultaneously.
3. Arrange seasoned eggs and bacon on the plate.
4. Season with salt and pepper, and garnish with fresh parsley. Serve with piping-hot eggs and bacon.

2. Steak and Eggs

Keep things simple with steak and eggs! Combine your favorite steak with eggs cooked to perfection.

Serving Size: 2

Duration: 25 minutes

Ingredients:

For the Eggs and steak:

- 6 oz. bone-in rib-eye/sirloin steak
- Salt and freshly ground black pepper

- 2 tbsp. unsalted butter
- 2 big free-range eggs

For the optional Chimichurri Steak Garnish:

- ¼ c. chopped flat-leaf parsley
- A few red pepper flakes
- ¼ c. virgin olive oil
- ¼ c. chopped oregano
- 4 sprigs of fresh mint
- Juice of ½ lime
- 2 garlic cloves minced
- Salt and freshly ground black pepper

Instruction:

For the Chimichurri:

1. In a medium mixing bowl, combine all of the ingredients. Set aside the proteins after they have finished cooking.

For the Steak and Eggs:

1. In a large cast-iron skillet over medium-high heat, melt the butter. Arrange the steak on one side of the grill, leaving room for the eggs.
2. Cook for 3 to 4 minutes on each side for a medium-rare steak or until the meat has a dark brown sear.
3. If the pan begins to dry out, add another tablespoon of butter. After lowering the heat, add the eggs.
4. Season with salt and pepper to taste. Cover the skillet with a lid and cook the egg whites for another 2 to 3 minutes or until they start to set.
5. Season the meat with salt and pepper before serving it with the eggs.
6. Serve with or without the chimichurri sauce.

3. Sausage and Eggs

What could be better for breakfast than hot, crispy sausages with scrambled eggs? Because it is high in nutrition, this is an excellent meal to prepare when running late for work.

Serving Size: 1

Ingredients:

- 2 tbsp. Butter
- 2 sausages
- A pinch of salt
- 2 eggs

Instructions:

1. Bring some water to a boil. Allow 8-10 minutes in boiling water after adding the eggs.
2. Grill or fry the sausages while the eggs are boiling. Remove the eggs from the water and peel them.
3. Scramble the eggs with a fork, then add the butter and salt.
4. Slice the sausages into small pieces. Dig into the mashed eggs with sausages!

4. Ham and Eggs

The American staple pairing of ham and cheese is popular. Sadly, ham and egg dishes don't have the same popularity but are fantastic. They are as delectable and versatile as ham and cheese. You may prepare omelets, burritos, ham and egg breakfasts, and more!

Total Time: 20 minutes

Servings: 4

Ingredients:

- 8 eggs, beaten
- ¼ tsp. seasoned salt
- 3 tbsp. milk
- 1 jalapeno pepper, seeded and minced
- Salt and ground black pepper
- ¼ c. olive oil
- ½ c. chopped deli slices Applewood-smoked ham
- 1 c. finely shredded Cheddar cheese, divided

Instruction:

1. Mix the eggs, milk, seasoned salt, and black pepper in a bowl.
2. Heat the olive oil in a large nonstick skillet over medium-high heat for two to three minutes or until the jalapeno pepper softens. Cook for about a minute, or until the ham is cooked through, with the jalapeno.
3. Pour the egg mixture into the ham mixture. Cook for 3-5 minutes or until the eggs are set but not dry. Sprinkle half of the cheddar cheese over the eggs; cook and stir until the cheese is melted. Then, on a plate, top the eggs with the remaining cheese.

Creative Carnivore Breakfast Recipes

1. Breakfast Steak Burrito

This dish may be prepared in only 20 minutes without sacrificing any flavor. The meal is "customizable" and contains fresh, juicy steak in every bite!

Ingredients:

- ½ c. prepared salsa
- ½ c. water
- ¼ c. instant brown rice
- 1 15-ounce can of black beans, low-sodium, rinsed
- 12 oz. steak, thinly sliced crosswise
- ¼ tsp. newly ground pepper
- 2 tbsp. chopped fresh cilantro
- 1 tbsp. canola oil
- ½ c. shredded Cheddar cheese
- 4 8-inch tortillas, whole-wheat preferred
- ¼ c. prepared guacamole

Instructions:

1. Bring salsa and water to a boil in a small saucepan.
2. Reduce to low heat, cover, and cook for 5 minutes.
3. Return to a simmer and cook for 5 minutes, uncovered, or until the rice is tender and most liquid has been absorbed.
4. Meanwhile, season the meat with pepper. Heat the oil in a large skillet over medium-high heat. Cook, occasionally tossing, for 3-5 minutes or until the steak is browned and cooked.
5. Divide the steak between the tortillas and top with an equal amount of cheese, guacamole, cilantro, and rice mixture. Each tortilla should be used to make a burrito.

2. Carnivore Omelet

In just 15 minutes, you can finish cooking a carnivorous omelet with various topping options. You name it—cheese, bacon, yogurt! So, don't restrict the enjoyment to only the morning; enjoy the high-protein breakfast anytime.

Ingredients:

- 4 large Eggs
- 50 g. Greek Yogurt
- 1 piece Bacon
- 50 g. 20% Beef Mince / Ground
- 20 g. Mozzarella Cheese
- 20 g. Salami
- ½ tsp. Himalayan Sea Salt

Instructions:

1. Brown the mince and bacon in a skillet heated to medium heat with some light oil. Meanwhile, beat the eggs.
2. After the meat has finished cooking, remove them and add the eggs.

3. Tilt the pan occasionally to help the runny portions settle in the center. Once the egg has started to firm up, add the toppings.
4. Cook for a few minutes more, then remove, fold, and serve.

3. Bacon and Egg Breakfast Salad

Eggs are abundant in protein and strong in minerals, vitamins, and antioxidants. Hence, if consumed in moderation, bacon and eggs may be a healthy breakfast meal.

Ingredients:

- 1 tsp. garlic oil
- 4 eggs
- 1 head escarole/frisee/other bitter leaves of choice
- 7 oz. smoked lardoons or about 14 slices of smoked bacon (cut into chunks)
- A dash of Worcestershire sauce
- 1 tsp. Dijon mustard
- 4 tsp. cider vinegar
- Small bunch of flat-leaf parsley, chop leaves

Instructions:

1. Boil the eggs in a saucepan of water over medium heat. Bring to a boil, cook for one minute, then remove from heat and set aside for ten minutes.
2. Chill the eggs in a dish of ice water. Peel the eggs once they are cool to the touch.
3. Meanwhile, tear the salad leaves into bite-sized pieces and place them in a serving bowl.
4. Heat the oil in a small frying pan over medium heat. Fry the lardons or bacon for 5 minutes or until crisp. Transfer the lardons or bacon to a plate lined with paper towels to drain while you make the dressing.
5. After whisking together the Dijon mustard and bacon juices in the pan, add the vinegar and a dab of Worcestershire sauce. Re-whisk the dressing before pouring it over the salad greens and tossing to combine.
6. Combine the eggs with the chopped parsley, add the lardons, and mix again. When gently mixing the ingredients, do not break up the eggs.
7. Hard-boiled eggs can be made four days ahead of time. Cool, keep the shells on, and store them in an airtight container in the fridge. Remove the shells just before serving.

4. Chorizo and Egg Breakfast Bowl

Breakfast bowls are fantastic, but many dishes can leave you hungry and wanting more. The ultimate comfort food meal is these chorizo breakfast bowls. This breakfast bowl is loaded with protein-rich quinoa, savory chorizo, fluffy eggs, and any toppings you like.

Ingredients:

- 1 tbsp. olive oil
- 1 c. quinoa
- 4 large eggs, lightly beaten
- 4 oz. chorizo see notes

- ½ c. diced yellow onion
- 2 garlic cloves minced
- 1 c. diced Roma tomatoes or your favorite tomatoes

Instructions:

1. In a large saucepan, cook the quinoa according to the package directions.
2. Over medium heat, heat the olive oil. Add the scrambled eggs when the olive oil is hot and cook until done. After removing from the pan, place on a plate.
3. Raise the heat to medium-high and cook the onions and garlic for 1 to 2 minutes or until tender.
4. Cook for 5 to 7 minutes, stirring frequently, until the chorizo is thoroughly cooked. If necessary, drain any excess fat.
5. Assemble the breakfast bowls.
6. Place an equal amount of quinoa in each dish, followed by eggs and tomatoes.
7. If desired, top with additional toppings.

Breakfast Meal Planning and Preparation Tips

Meal planning and preparation are valuable skills to have in your toolbox for health and wellness. A well-planned meal plan can assist you in meeting a specific health goal or improving your diet's quality while saving you time and money.

This section contains some excellent advice on how to eat a healthy breakfast while still getting enough sleep. Finally, here are some lovely recipes that are great for meal planning! But first, it should be stated why breakfast is so important and why it should always be included in your morning routine.

Why is a Nutritious Breakfast So Crucial?

As you may already know, breakfast is the most important meal. Our bodies consume most of the calories required for our basic metabolism at night, leaving us with a half-empty energy tank in the morning.

As a result, eating a balanced breakfast in the morning is even more important. A healthy carbohydrate energy boost is the best way to start your day. Only then will your muscles, organs, and brain function properly!

If you start the day with a healthy breakfast, your blood sugar level will remain stable. As a result, you won't have to deal with rabid food cravings or uncontrollable sweet desires. It will also be easier for you to maintain your weight or lose a few pounds.

What is Meal Preparation?

The cooking or preparation of meals is referred to as meal prep. And finishing this in a single day for the entire week is preferable!

You can prepare individual ingredients to make later meal preparation easier or precook entire dishes and freeze portions.

Benefits of Meal Prepping

You'll be surprised at how much time meal prep can save you. Not only is your breakfast ready when you wake up, but you also don't have to go grocery shopping as often. If you plan ahead of time, you will avoid purchasing unnecessary food that spoils in the refrigerator. Also, because you won't have to buy breakfast on your way to work, you'll be able to save money more easily.

Tips to Help Meal Preparation

Correctly Combine the Ingredients

You already know that your breakfast should include carbohydrates, proteins, and lipids. However, selecting the right food combinations for breakfast is equally important. Nothing can stop you from having a productive and active day if you keep these healthy combinations in mind.

Make Use of the Right Containers

After preparing your breakfast dishes, place them in storage-friendly containers. This frees up space in your refrigerator for additional food and makes it easier for you to navigate. Light containers are also useful for bringing your breakfast to work.

Choose the Appropriate Ingredients

Your various breakfast options are an excellent place to begin! Ingredients make a huge difference in the quality of a meal.

Nuts should always be present in a nutritious breakfast. Because they are high in plant-based protein and contain beneficial fats, they are a good source of protein.

How to Meal Prep for the Week

Food Planning

The most important step in preparing healthy meals for the entire week is unquestionably meal planning. Create a weekly schedule as follows:

A thorough meal plan, unsurprisingly, includes a grocery list. As you have undoubtedly seen, you can enter the food you already have at home and should eat. You can simply reduce food waste while using leftovers in delightful and inventive ways by doing so!

Get Organized

Any good meal plan must have a solid organizational foundation.

An organized kitchen, pantry, and refrigerator make everything from creating menus to grocery shopping and meal preparation a breeze because you'll know exactly what you have on hand and where your equipment and materials are.

You can organize your meal prep areas however you want. But make sure it's a system that works for you.

Make Preparations For and Use Leftovers

If you don't want to spend time cooking every day of the week, plan to make enough food to have leftovers.

Making a few extra servings of whatever you're making for dinner is a great, easy way to prepare for tomorrow's lunch.

If you don't like leftovers, think about using them differently so they don't taste like leftovers.

For example, if you roast a whole chicken with herbs or vegetables for supper, you can use the leftover chicken the next day for lunch by shredding it and adding it to tacos or salad.

Portion Meals in Advance

Pre-portioning your meals into individual containers is a great meal prep technique, especially if you're trying to consume a certain amount of food.

This technique is frequently used by athletes and fitness enthusiasts who closely monitor their calorie and nutrient intake. It's also a great way to promote weight loss when you're short on time.

To reap the benefits of this technique, prepare a substantial dinner with at least 4-6 servings. Place each dish in its container and keep it chilled or frozen. Simply reheat and serve as desired.

Modify Your Menu

Getting into a diet rut and eating the same foods daily is easy.

Your meals may quickly become monotonous, causing you to lose your creative spark for cooking. At worst, a lack of diversity may result in nutrient deficiencies.

To avoid this, try to experiment with different foods or meals regularly.

If you always choose chicken, try switching to fish or bacon. If you normally eat salad, try replacing it with some meat sausage.

You might also consider allowing the seasons to change your menu. Seasonal produce allows you to vary your diet while saving money.

Use the Freezer

Cooking specific dishes or meals in bulk and freezing them for later use can help you save time, reduce waste, and stretch your food budget.

Bulk Purchases

Use the bulk section of your local supermarket to save money, buy only what you need, and reduce wasteful packaging.

A great place to stock up on pantry staples like quinoa, seeds, almonds, dried fruit, and beans. Bring your containers if you don't want to use plastic bags to transport your bulk purchases home.

Bulk Cook

Batch cooking occurs when you prepare various meals in large quantities to use them in various ways throughout the week. This strategy will be useful if you don't have much time to cook during the week.

Consider making a large batch of quinoa or fish at the start of the week and roasting a large tray of vegetables, tofu, or meat to use in salads, scrambles, or grain bowls later in the week.

Prepare a batch of chicken, tuna, or chickpea salad for salads, crackers, or sandwiches.

Quick and Easy Breakfast Ideas for Busy Mornings

While a pure Carnivore Diet focuses solely on meat, the dishes in this section provide some variety. Some ingredients listed in the recipes are optional, depending on your diet's restrictions.

Moderations can be used as usual based on personal preferences. We are constantly looking for the newest and best recipes that will allow you to follow a carnivore diet.

1. Carnivore Breakfast Pizza

Everyone enjoys pizza, right? It is incredibly simple to make, full of flavor and protein.

Ingredients:

- 1 Carnivore Flatbread baked in a 13×11-inch rectangle or oval
- A dash of salt
- ½ c. heavy cream
- 1 clove of garlic pressed or minced
- ½ c. shredded cheese mozzarella, cheddar, or gouda
- ½ c. sour cream
- 3 slices of bacon chopped and pan-fried

Instructions:

1. Bake the Carnivore Flatbread in a 13 x 11-inch rectangle or oval pan. After removing the baking sheet from the oven, leave it lined. Preheat the oven to 415°F.
2. Combine the heavy cream, garlic, and salt in a small bowl. Then stir in the cheese. Spread the ingredients on the pizza crust and add bacon on top.
3. Bake the pizza for 15 minutes or until the cheese is melted. Refrigerate any leftovers in an airtight container.

Notes:

- This crust is simple to make ahead of time. Make the pizza crust the night before and bake it for breakfast. Finally, all that remains to be done in the morning is to top it and bake it!
- Crispy bacon enhances the flavor of this morning's pizza, but other meats also work well. You may substitute cooked breakfast sausage, chopped deli ham, or a variety of meats.

2. Carnivore Breakfast Sandwich

A breakfast sandwich is a tried-and-true favorite. This breakfast sandwich is full of flavor, high in protein and fat, and will keep you satisfied for the rest of the day. Instead of a carb, two sausage patties are used as the structure to keep the egg and cheddar cheese inside. Don't be shy if you're looking for a quick Carnivorous breakfast idea!

Ingredients:

- 1 egg
- 2 Beef Sausage Patties
- 1 tsp. butter/bacon grease, if you have it
- 1 oz. cheddar cheese

Instructions:

1. In a large skillet over medium heat, melt the butter. Form the sausage into thin patties about half an inch thick and the size of your palm. Fry patties until golden on one side, then flip and cook for two to three minutes or until done.
2. If it doesn't bother you, fry 1 egg in the same pan as the rest of your ingredients. If not, assemble your carnivore breakfast sandwich in a

separate pan with more butter. Keep the sauce and yolk runny. Place 1 sausage patty, a fried egg, a slice of cheese, and another sausage patty on a platter.

3. Enjoy! Sautéed spinach, tomato, or avocado slices could also be added.

3. Keto Carnivore Waffle

You crave variety occasionally when it comes to a strict, high-protein, low-carb diet like the ketogenic or carnivore diet. This carnivore diet adaptation of a classic breakfast recipe will quickly become a favorite.

Ingredients:

- 1 egg
- ⅓ c. mozzarella cheese
- ½ c. ground pork rinds
- 1 pinch of salt

Instructions:

1. Preheat the waffle maker to medium-high temperature. Combine the egg, cheese, ground pork rinds, and salt in a mixing bowl.
2. Adding ingredients to a carnivorous waffle

3. Spoon the pancake on top of the waffle. After 3-5 minutes of cooking in a closed waffle machine, the waffles should be golden brown and firm. Remove the pancake from the waffle maker and serve it to yourself.

Tips for Cooking the Perfect Steak or Bacon

The most important step in cooking a steak is choosing the right and healthy meat. Nothing can be done to improve the flavor of a bad, flavorless steak. The goal is to highlight the meat's distinct, mouthwatering essence. Given that you're starting with some delectable grass-fed steaks straight from the farm, here are the top ten suggestions:

A Cold Steak Must Not Be Cooked

Allow your steak to come to room temperature before cooking to ensure even cooking. It is best to leave a steak out for about an hour before cooking.

Avoid Seasoning Your Steak Too Much

Salting is an important step in seasoning. Salt releases the natural flavors of steak and moisture from the meat's muscles. Some chefs recommend adding salt when the meat is removed from the refrigerator. This may not be important but don't wait until the last minute to season your food.

Chefs season with salt, black pepper, and occasionally garlic. You want the meat's delicious flavor to shine through.

Choose a Suitable Cooking Oil

Because of its low smoke point, olive oil constantly smokes (300 degrees). Avocado, soybean, and canola oils are the best cooking oils for steak because they all have high smoke points ranging from 400 to 520 degrees. Clarified butter with a smoke point of 450 degrees is another option.

A Good Pan Should Be Used, and It Should Be Very Hot

Many steakhouses now use infrared broilers for cooking their steaks evenly and at extremely high temperatures. Unfortunately, most of us cannot access such high-end cooking equipment at home. Cast iron skillets are ideal for proper searing and caramelization because they retain heat. Because cast iron is a thick metal, it allows for even heat distribution. As a result, the steak is evenly browned and cooked.

Avoid Overcooking Your Steak

When my daughter recently confided in me that she was nervous about making some ribeyes, I reassured her that the only thing she could do very badly was overcook it.

It can be difficult to avoid overcooking because the thickness of the cut and the temperature of the grill or skillet determine how quickly your steak cooks. You can cut the steak to see if it's done, but it may be dangerous because it releases juices.

Make use of a meat thermometer. Meat thermometers are inserted into the flesh's core to determine its internal temperature. They are available in both digital and analog formats. For a medium-rare steak, the temperature should be between 125 and 130°F. However, because the steak will continue to cook on the plate, it should be removed from the heat source when it is 5°F below the required temperature.

Do Not Be Concerned with the Number of Times You Flip Your Steak

You've probably heard that frequently flipping a steak is a bad idea. Renowned chefs advise not to be concerned and suggest that flipping it frequently may improve the outcome by cooking more evenly through the center.

Serve the Steak After It Has Rested

You create a crust that traps moisture when you cook a steak on a hot grill or in a hot skillet. If you bite into your steak right after it comes off the grill, you risk losing all of its delicious liquids. Thinner steaks should rest for five to seven minutes, while heavier slices of beef should rest for at least ten minutes. A meat thermometer can determine whether your steak has rested long enough. The ideal temperature for the center of a steak, regardless of thickness, is 120°F.

Serve On a Warm Plate and Cut Against the Grain

The presentation of a steak can have a significant impact on its flavor, texture, and visual appeal, as well as its overall appeal. If you want to slice the meat before serving, always cut against the grain or perpendicular to the direction of the muscle fibers. Because muscle fibers can be tough, cutting through them will make the beef more tender. Cutting through the muscle fibers, on the other hand, will have the opposite effect.

Another tip for improving your home dining experience is to warm the dish before serving. A warm plate helps maintain the food's temperature, whereas a cold plate absorbs the heat and can produce a lukewarm steak. One of the best ways to warm your plates is to stack them in a low-temperature oven or place them on a stovetop burner.

Chapter 6: Carnivore Recipes

Chicken

1. Fried Chicken

Chicken pieces are breaded and fried in hot oil until golden brown.

Total Time: 50 min

Yield: 16 pieces

Ingredients:

- 6 c. all-purpose flour
- Vegetable oil for frying
- 2 whole free-range, organic chickens

- 2 tsp. cayenne pepper
- 4 tbsp. ground black pepper
- 2 tbsp. garlic powder
- 5 tbsp. salt
- 1 tbsp. onion powder
- 2 c. buttermilk

Instructions:

1. Separate two whole chickens into four breasts, thighs, legs, and wings.
2. Preheat your oil to 325 degrees F in a deep fryer or a big stovetop pan.
3. Add the flour, salt, black pepper, garlic powder, onion powder, and cayenne pepper in a large mixing bowl. Place aside.
4. Place the buttermilk in a separate basin large enough to accommodate the chicken.
5. Prepare your dredging station. Place your chicken in a bowl. The buttermilk basin should be next to the dry mixture.
6. Lightly dust the chicken breasts with the flour mixture before dipping them in the buttermilk and covering them well.
7. Firmly press the flour mixture into the wet chicken breasts while holding the breasts in the flour mixture. The appropriate crust and crunch will not be obtained if the coating is not thoroughly applied. Carefully place the breasts in the hot oil.
8. Repeat the dredging procedures with the remaining chicken, starting with the thigh, then the leg, and finally, the wing.
9. When you add the last wing to the fryer, there should be 16 pieces of chicken in the oil. Set a timer for 15 minutes.
10. After 15 minutes, use a probe thermometer to check the temperature of a breast. If the thermometer reads 180 degrees F, your chicken is done. Remember that it will continue to cook after you remove it from

the fryer. Set your chicken aside and let it drain for five minutes. Let cool before serving.

2. Chicken Alfredo

Pasta is tossed with a sauce made of cream, Parmesan cheese, and garlic and then topped with grilled chicken.

Ingredients:

- 1 ½ c. whole milk
- 2 tbsp. extra-virgin olive oil
- Kosher salt
- Twp cloves garlic, minced
- Freshly ground black pepper
- 1 ½ c. low-sodium chicken broth
- 1 c. freshly grated Parmesan
- Two boneless chicken breasts
- 8 oz. fettuccine
- ½ c. heavy cream
- Freshly chopped parsley

Instructions:

1. In a large skillet, heat the oil over medium-high heat. Season with salt and pepper to taste. Fry for 8 minutes per side or until golden and cooked through. Slice after 10 minutes of rest.
2. Combine the milk, broth, and garlic in a skillet. Cook the food after adding salt and pepper. Cook for 3 minutes, stirring regularly, after adding the fettuccine. Allow for another 8 minutes of simmering.
3. Stir in the heavy cream and Parmesan cheese. Simmer until the sauce thickens.
4. Remove from the heat and stir in the chicken slices. Garnish with parsley.

3. BBQ Chicken

Set your chicken aside and let it drain for five minutes. Let cool before serving.

Marinated chicken is grilled or baked with BBQ sauce. If done correctly, it will take at least an hour, if not two hours. Remember that, unlike grilling, which is hot and fast, BBQ is slow and low. Grilling a chicken breast is OK, but grilling chicken thighs, legs, or wings is preferable.

As a result, managing body heat in whatever way you can is critical. Place the chicken on the top rack of the grill, away from the heat, or if using a gas grill, just reduce the heat to low. You'll have a cool place either way. The greatest BBQ chicken is made slowly.

Total Time: 110 minutes

Servings: 4 to 6 servings

Ingredients:

- Kosher salt
- 4 lb. bone-in, skin-on chicken legs, wings, thighs, breasts
- 1 c. barbecue sauce, homemade or store-bought
- Vegetable oil or Extra virgin olive oil

Instructions:

1. Set your chicken aside and let it drain for five minutes. Let cool before serving.
2. Season and oil the chicken pieces. The chicken pieces should be coated in olive oil and seasoned on all sides.
3. Preheat the grill. Set your grill to high; direct heat on one side. If you're using charcoal or wood, ensure the grill has a cold side with few to no embers.
4. Move the seared chicken to the cool side of the grill. Place the chicken pieces, skin side down, on the hotter side of the grill to sear the skin. Cook for 5 to 10 minutes without a cover to avoid scorching, depending on the grill's hotness.
5. Turn the chicken pieces over and place them on the cooler side of the grill once they have a decent sear on one side. Set your chicken aside and let it drain for five minutes. Let cool before serving.
6. If using a gas grill, move the chicken pieces to the colder side, away from the flame, and keep the flame only on one side of the grill. Reduce the temperature to low or medium-low (250°F to 275°F).
7. Cook the grill, covered and without stirring, for 20 to 30 minutes. Cook, turn, and baste until done. Turn the chicken pieces over and baste with your favorite barbecue sauce. Cover the grill and cook for another 15 to 20 minutes.
8. Continue to flip the chicken pieces over, baste with sauce, cover the pan, and simmer for 10 to 30 minutes more. Set your chicken aside and let it drain for five minutes. Let cool before serving.
9. The timing will vary based on how your grill is set up, the size of your chicken pieces, and how chilly they start. Smaller pieces of chicken may finish cooking faster on a charcoal grill. The goal is to maintain the grill temperature low enough for the chicken to cook.

10. The internal temperature of the chicken pieces should be 160°F for the breasts and 170°F for the thighs when measured using a meat thermometer. The chicken is also done if the fluids flow clear when a knife is placed into the thickest chunk.
11. Set your chicken aside and let it drain for five minutes. Let cool before serving. If the chicken hasn't finished cooking, turn it over and maintain the heat low.
12. Finish with a last sear on the hot side of the grill before removing it from the heat, if desired. Place the meat on the hot side of the grill, skin side down, to achieve this. Allow them to sear and blacken for a minute or two. Brush on more barbecue sauce to the grilled chicken before serving.

4. Chicken Parmesan

Breaded chicken cutlets are fried and baked with tomato sauce and mozzarella cheese.

Ingredients:

- 4 boneless, skinless chicken breast halves
- 2 large eggs
- Freshly ground black pepper and salt to taste
- ¾ c. grated Parmesan cheese, divided

- 1 c. or as required of panko bread crumbs,
- 2 tbsp. or as required for all-purpose flour
- ½ c. of prepared tomato sauce
- ½ c. or required of olive oil
- ¼ c. of chopped fresh basil
- 2 tsp. olive oil
- ¼ c. fresh mozzarella to be cut into small cubes
- ½ c. grated provolone cheese

Instructions:

1. Set your chicken aside and let it drain for five minutes. Let cool before serving. Preheat the oven to 450 degrees F.
2. Place chicken breasts between two sheets of heavy plastic on a stable, flat surface. (resealable freezer bags work nicely). Pound the chicken until it is ½-inch thick with a meat mallet's smooth side.
3. Season chicken liberally with salt and pepper. Using a sifter or strainer, evenly coat both sides of the chicken breasts with flour. Whisk the eggs in a separate bowl and leave aside.
4. Mix ½ cup Parmesan cheese with the bread crumbs in a separate bowl and set aside. Set your chicken aside and let it drain for five minutes. Let cool before serving.
5. A flour-coated chicken breast is brushed with beaten eggs. Place the breast in the breadcrumb mixture, pressing crumbs into both sides. Repeat for each breast. Allow the chicken to rest for 10 to 15 minutes.
6. Heat ½ inch olive oil in a big skillet over medium-high heat until it shims. Fry the chicken in the hot oil for two minutes on each side or until browned. The chicken will finish cooking in the oven.

7. Set your chicken aside and let it drain for five minutes. Let cool before serving. Season chicken liberally with salt and pepper. Using a sifter or strainer, evenly coat both sides of the chicken breasts with flour.
8. Whisk the eggs in a separate bowl and leave aside. Mix ½ cup Parmesan cheese with the bread crumbs in a separate bowl and set aside.
9. A flour-coated chicken breast is brushed with beaten eggs. Place the breast in the breadcrumb mixture, pressing crumbs into both sides. Repeat for each breast. Allow the chicken to rest for 10 to 15 minutes.
10. Heat ½ inch olive oil in a big skillet over medium-high heat until it shims. Fry the chicken in the hot oil for two minutes on each side or until browned.

5. Roast Chicken

A whole chicken is roasted in the oven with herbs and spices.

Ingredients:

- Kosher salt
- 1 (5-6 pound) roasting chicken
- 1 lemon halved
- Freshly ground black pepper
- 1 large bunch of fresh thyme and 20 sprigs
- 1 head of garlic, cut in half crosswise
- Olive oil
- 1 large yellow onion
- 2 tbsp. butter melted
- 4 carrots cut into 2-inch chunks
- 1 bulb of fennel, cut into wedges

Instructions:

1. Preheat the oven to 425 degrees Fahrenheit.

2. Remove the chicken giblets. Rinse the bird from head to toe. Pat the outside dry after removing any excess fat and pin feathers. Season the inside of the chicken well with salt and pepper. Insert the garlic clove, thyme sprig, and two lemon halves into the cavity.
3. Season the skin of the chicken with salt and pepper one more time. Secure the chicken's legs with kitchen twine, then tuck the wing tips beneath the body. Place the fennel, onions, and carrots in a roasting pan.
4. Toss with 20 thyme sprigs, olive oil, salt, and pepper. Place the chicken on top of the mixture evenly distributed throughout the pan.
5. After roasting the bird for 1 ½ hours, the juices should run clear when you cut between a leg and a thigh. Remove the chicken and veggies from the dish and wrap them in aluminum foil for about 20 minutes. On a serving plate, arrange the vegetables and cut the chicken.

Pork

1. Pork Chops

Pork chops are grilled or pan-fried until cooked through.

Cook Time: 1 hour

Servings: 2

Ingredients:

- ½ c. pancetta
- 4 tbsp. (around 60g) of butter, cut into 8 portions
- Two thick pork chops
- 1 skillet

Instructions:

1. To begin, preheat your oven to 450°F (230°C). While the oven is heating up, put crisp half-diced pancetta in a frying pan. Remove from the heat and set aside to cool sufficiently to handle. Wait until you've washed the skillet.
2. Using a very sharp knife, cut a "pocket" along the length of each pork chop. Following that, the pocket will be filled with pancetta. Allow at least 14 inches on the backside and either end of the chop.
3. Stuff the pocket with the cooked pancetta and two butter pads. Place each chop in the same frying pan used to crisp the pancetta.
4. Arrange the extra uncooked pancetta around the chops and fry in the remaining butter. Carefully place everything in the oven.
5. After 45 minutes, remove the pan from the oven and pour the excess grease into a container for later use.
6. Return the meat to the hot oven for 10 minutes to increase color.
7. Serve and enjoy.

2. Pork Ribs

Pork ribs are slow-cooked with BBQ sauce until tender. These delicious baby back ribs will satisfy everyone in the family. You may be as strict a carnivore as you like with the spices.

Ingredients:

- 1 tbsp. paprika
- 2 tbsp. kosher salt
- 1 tbsp. chili powder
- 1 rack of baby back pork ribs
- 1 ½ tsp. cayenne pepper
- 1 c. beef broth
- 2 tsp. garlic powder
- 1 tsp. ground black pepper
- ¼ c. barbeque sauce, or as needed

Instructions:

1. Combine salt, chili powder, paprika, garlic powder, cayenne pepper, and black pepper in a small bowl for the spice rub.
2. Cut the rack of ribs into four equal pieces. Apply spice rub to the whole surface of each piece.
3. Pour the broth into a multifunctional pressure cooker.
4. Cut the ribs into a teepee shape. Close the lid to secure it. Set the timer for 30 minutes and use high pressure according to the manufacturer's instructions. Allow 10 to 15 minutes for the pressure to build.
5. Preheat the oven to 425 degrees F. Cover a baking sheet with aluminum foil.
6. Following the manufacturer's instructions, use the quick-release technique to slowly relieve the pressure, which should take around 5 minutes. The lock and lid have been removed. Transfer the ribs to the baking sheet with tongs. The ribs should be slathered in BBQ sauce all over.
7. Bake in a preheated oven for 7 minutes. Turn the ribs over after 7 minutes and continue roasting until the meat easily separates from the

bone. An instant-read thermometer should read 145 degrees Fahrenheit inside the house. (63 degrees C).

3. Ham

A cured and roasted leg of a pig that is commonly served on holidays. It's a one-pot keto dinner that takes around 30 minutes to prepare.

Ingredients:

- 2 c. bone broth (or regular broth)
- 2 c. cheddar cheese, grated (save ½ cup for garnish)
- 2 oz. cream cheese cut into small pieces
- 10-12 oz. cubed cooked ham
- Salt and Pepper to taste, depending on your broth
- 1 c. Carnivore Noodles (optional)
- ½ c. heavy cream
- ¼ c. bacon crumbles

Instructions:

1. In a thick medium soup, heat the broth until it almost reaches a simmer. Keep the broth on low heat.

2. Whisk the cream cheese cubes into the soup, then mix until all lumps are gone.
3. Stir in the grated cheese, ½ cup at a time, until it melts into the mixture.
4. Cubed ham and noodles should be added and cooked through on low heat.
5. Simmer for a further minute on low heat after gently adding heavy cream.
6. Divide the mixture into four big bowls, then top with grated cheddar cheese and saved bacon or bacon crumbles.

Notes:
- Making this soup with items you already have is a wonderful idea.
- You can make this ahead of time by cutting leftover ham or pork roast.
- You can use this recipe to make bone broth or any carton of beef broth you have on hand.

4. Bacon

Strips of pork belly that are cured and fried until crispy.

Total Time: 1hr

Number of Servings: 3

Ingredients:

- Spring onions
- 500 g. pork belly
- 1 tbsp. Kosher salt for the meat
- ¼ tsp. black pepper
- 1 tsp. soy sauce
- ½ tsp. ground ginger
- ½ tsp. olive oil

- Freshly chopped cilantro

Instructions:

1. Make as many holes in the pig's skin as possible without penetrating the meat with a metal skewer.
2. Using a sharp knife, cut the skin into 1-inch strips.
3. Combine water, salt, spring onions, ginger, and black pepper in a large pot. Cook for at least 40 to 60 minutes on medium heat after adding the pork belly meat.
4. When all the water has been drained, place the pig meat on a surface covered with paper towels to air dry. After that, cut it into bite-sized strips.
5. Fry pork belly with soy sauce in a hot skillet with oil until it is as crisp as you like.
6. For a different flavor, add more spices or Chinese cooking wine here.
7. Serve your crispy, fried pork belly immediately with your favorite side dish after garnishing it with fresh cilantro.

5. Sausages

Ground pork is seasoned and formed into links, then grilled or fried.

Total Time: 2 hours

Servings: 20

Ingredients:

- 40 g. kosher salt
- ¼ c. sherry vinegar
- 4 lb. pork shoulder
- 1 lb. pork fat
- 6 g. cracked black pepper
- 35 g. sugar
- 1 c. minced fresh parsley
- ¾ c. dry sherry
- 20 g. toasted fennel seeds
- 4 g. ground nutmeg
- 1 head of garlic, peeled and chopped

Special Equipment:

- Kitchen scale
- Hog casings
- Meat grinder having coarse and fine dies
- Sausage stuffer

Instructions:

1. Before you begin, ensure all your ingredients are ready, and the meat and fat are very cold (you can put your meat and fat in the freezer for 2 hours). Place the bowls and grinder in the freezer or refrigerator for an hour before using them.
2. Cut the fat and meat into small pieces and refrigerate in an ice-filled bowl. On top of a large bowl of prepared ice, place a medium metal

bowl. Cut the meat and fat into an inch to two inches-wide pieces. Fat should be cut somewhat finer than meat.

3. To keep your components cold, place the sliced beef and fat in a bowl in a larger basin filled with ice. Combine the meat and fat as soon as they are sliced. Refrigerate after adding the majority of the spices.

4. Pour in the bulk of your spices and blend quickly. After adding the salt and sugar, repeat the mixing procedure.

5. Place the sausage mixture in the freezer for at least 30 minutes and no more than an hour, either in a closed container or wrapped in plastic wrap.

6. Because sherry is not commonly used in Italian sausage, mix the dry sherry and sherry vinegar before chilling. You can use white wine and white wine vinegar if you like.

7. If you intend to stuff your sausage, take some casings (15 to 18 feet for a batch of 5-pound links) and soak them in warm water. You can skip this step if you don't want to stuff your sausage.

8. Set up the grinder. Use the coarse die for Italian sausage, although either would work. Avoid using a very fine die because the meat must be crushed coarsely first, then refrozen, and then processed again with the fine die. Furthermore, Italian sausage is intended to be unpolished.

9. Chill the sausage mixture once it has been ground. Push the sausage mixture through the grinder as quickly as possible. Make sure the ground beef is placed in a cold basin.

10. After you've ground all of the beef, place it in the freezer and clean up the area and grinder. After removing the mixture, add the remaining spices and sherry vinegar combination.

11. Using a stand mixer's paddle attachment, a large wooden spoon, or your clean hands, thoroughly combine the sausage. Allow 90 seconds on level 1 of a stand mixer. Using your hands or a spoon may take a

little longer. Like when you knead bread, you want the mixture to become sticky and begin to adhere to itself.

12. The sausage will be ready after it is completed. To cook, take a scoop and roll it into a ball using your hands. Spread your wings a little. Cook for 5 to 10 minutes on each side in a pan over medium-low heat or until browned and done.

Beef

1. Hamburgers

Ground beef patties are prepared and grilled or fried. Please use fatty ground beef with no more than 80% lean meat to make excellent and juicy hamburger patties.

Ingredients:

- 1½ tsp. sea salt
- 2 lb. ground beef

Instructions:

1. Bring the ground beef to room temperature. Spread the ground beef on a tray or large chopping board, season with salt, and gently mix.

Some people recommend sprinkling salt on hamburger patties shortly before cooking to keep the meat from drying out.

2. Combine the salt and other seasonings before forming them to ensure the burgers are evenly seasoned.
3. Divide the ground beef into 8 equal parts. Each one should be rolled into a ball before being pressed into a burger patty form, or the top of a paper cup can be cut off and used as a mold.
4. Firmly push the ground beef piece into the mold to fill all the gaps. Using the mold, you may make uniform burger patties less likely to crumble when cooking.
5. Melt butter in a griddle pan or nonstick frying pan over medium-high heat. Ensure the pan is hot enough that when water drops on the surface, it evaporates immediately.
6. You can add a tablespoon of fat if you want, but it may not be necessary if you use fatty ground beef. Add two burger patties and keep the pan temperature high to evenly brown the patties.
7. Cook for 3 to 4 minutes. Please do not press down or move the burgers while they are cooking to avoid them from falling apart and achieve the proper level of browning, giving the burgers a great flavor.
8. It is better to handle them as little as possible. Grill for another 3 to 4 minutes for medium-rare or 5 minutes for medium after flipping the burgers using a big spatula. Cook for a few minutes longer if you prefer them well done.
9. Arrange the burgers on a dish and set them aside to rest. They should stay in the fridge for five days but must be consumed within a few days.

2. Steak

Beef is grilled or pan-fried to the desired doneness.

The Perfect Grilled Steak

Ingredients:

- 4 rib-eye steaks about 1 ½" thick, around 1 pound each
- 1 tsp. salt plus more for seasoning
- Pepper
- 1 tsp. cornstarch

Instructions:

- In a small bowl, combine the salt and cornstarch. After patting the steaks dry, rub the salt mixture on them.
- Place the steaks on a wire rack in the freezer for 30 to 1 hour to chill.
- In the meantime, start a fire on your charcoal grill and clean the grates for steak cooking. Season the steaks with pepper.
- On the grill, allow 4 to 8 minutes per side.
- Remove the grill and cover it with foil. Before serving, allow 5 minutes. To serve, slice thinly across the grain at an angle.

3. Roast Beef

A cut of beef is roasted in the oven until cooked through.

Roast Beef and Vegetables

Cook Time: 20 minutes

Servings: 3-4

Ingredients:

- Salt
- Freshly ground pepper
- 2 lb. Top rump of beef, room temperature
- 2 onions, peeled and chopped
- Olive oil for drizzling
- 2 tsp. thyme
- 1 lb. New potatoes, halved
- 1 bulb of garlic, broken into cloves and peeled
- 2 c. beef stock
- 3 carrots, peeled and chopped
- 2 bay leaves
- 2 sticks of celery, roughly chopped

Instructions:

1. Preheat oven to 425 degrees Fahrenheit. (220 C). Season the meat with salt, pepper, and thyme all over with a little olive oil.
2. In a cast iron skillet heated over high heat, sear the beef for 3–4 minutes on each side, turning it occasionally, until it is nicely browned but not scorched.
3. Arrange the vegetables and bay leaves in the bottom of a roasting pan. Drizzle the roast with olive oil and serve.
4. After baking the roast for about 15 minutes, reduce the oven temperature to 375 F. (190 C). Roast for 13-15 minutes for rare, 17-19 minutes for medium, and 22-25 minutes for cooked through.
5. Check the meat with a thermometer to ensure it is at the desired temperature (medium rare is 145°F, and medium is 160°F). While the

roast is cooking, baste it a couple of times and watch the vegetables. If they begin to burn, cover the pan with a foil tent.

6. Remove the beef from the oven and set it aside on a board, covered with foil and a kitchen towel, for 15 to 30 minutes. Remember that the meat will continue to cook while resting, so remove it from the oven when it is 5°F below the ideal temperature. If the veggies still need to be cooked while the meat rests, return them to the oven until they are.

4. Meatloaf

Ground beef is mixed with breadcrumbs, eggs, and spices, then baked in the oven.

Total Time: 1 hour 40 minutes

Servings: 8

Ingredients:

- ¾ c. milk
- 2 eggs, beaten
- 1 tsp. dry mustard
- ¼ c. finely chopped onion
- 2 tbsp. packed brown sugar
- ⅔ c. fine dry bread crumbs/2 c. soft bread crumbs
- 2 tbsp. Snipped fresh parsley
- ½ tsp. dried leaf sage, basil/oregano, crushed
- 1 tsp. salt
- 1 ½ lb. lean ground beef, lamb, or pork
- ⅛ tsp. black pepper
- ¼ c. ketchup

Instructions:

1. Mix eggs and milk in a medium bowl before adding bread crumbs, onion, parsley, salt, and pepper. Add in the ground beef. Blend gently with clean hands until well combined. Press the mixture gently into an 8x4x2-inch loaf pan.
2. Bake for 1 to 1-¼ hours at 350°F or until an internal thermometer registers 160°F. After combining ketchup, sugar, and mustard in a bowl, spread over meat. Bake for another 10 minutes. Allow 10 minutes of rest time before cutting into 8 slices.

5. Tacos

Beef is seasoned and served in a taco shell with toppings like cheese, lettuce, and salsa.

Ingredients:

- 1 tsp. chili powder
- 1 medium onion, chopped
- 1 lb. lean ground beef
- ½ tsp. salt
- 8 oz. tomato sauce
- ½ tsp. garlic powder
- 1 ½ c. shredded Cheddar cheese (6 oz)
- 4.6 oz. Old El Paso Crunchy Taco Shells (12 Count)

- 2 c. shredded lettuce
- ¾ c. Old El Paso Thick 'n Chunky salsa
- 2 medium tomatoes, chopped
- ¾ c. sour cream, if needed

Instructions:

1. Set the oven temperature to 250°F. Brown the ground beef and onion in a large skillet, constantly stirring, for 8 to 10 minutes or until thoroughly cooked.
2. Season with salt, garlic powder, and chili powder. Reduce the heat to low, cover the pot, and let it simmer for 10 minutes.
3. Place the taco shells on an ungreased cookie sheet. Cook for 5 minutes at 250°F.
4. Layer the meat mixture, cheese, lettuce, and tomatoes in each taco shell to build the tacos. Serve topped with salsa and sour cream.

Lamb

1. Grilled Lamb Chops

Lamb chops are marinated and then grilled until cooked through.

Cook Time: 12 minutes

Servings: 4

Ingredients:

- 1 tbsp. chopped fresh thyme leaves, and 1 large sprig
- 8 lamb loin or rib chops
- 1 tsp. freshly squeezed lemon juice
- ¼ tsp. freshly ground black pepper
- ½ c. dry white wine or low-sodium chicken broth

- 4 tbsp. unsalted butter, divided
- 1 large garlic clove smashed
- ¾ tsp. kosher salt, divided
- 1 small shallot, finely chopped
- 1 tbsp. Finely grated lemon zest

Instructions:

1. Season the lamb. After taking the lamb chops from the fridge, season with ½ teaspoon salt, ½ teaspoon pepper, and ½ teaspoon chopped thyme. Allow the lamb chops to come to room temperature for 5 minutes.
2. Get the lamb ready. Melt 2 tablespoons butter in a 12-inch skillet over medium-high heat. Cook for 4 to 6 minutes, or up to 10 minutes if using thicker lamb chops, or until a rich, brown crust forms on the bottom.
3. Change the lamb. Cook for another 4 to 6 minutes or until an instant-read thermometer inserted into the center of the lamb chops reads 145°F.
4. Arrange on a plate. Wrap the lamb chops in foil and place them on a plate. Pour away everything except 2 tablespoons of the rendered fat.
5. Sauté the thyme, shallot, and garlic in a skillet. The heat should be reduced to medium. Sauté the shallot, garlic, and thyme sprig for about a minute or until the onion softens and browns.
6. Deglaze the pan. Before deglazing with the wine, broth, and lemon juice, scrape any burnt bits off the pan's bottom.
7. Finish the sauce. Cook for 1 to 2 minutes or until the liquid has been reduced by half. Combine the remaining ¼ teaspoon salt, 2 tablespoons butter, and lemon zest in a mixing bowl. Simmer for about a minute or until the butter melts and the sauce thickens slightly. Taste and season

with salt and pepper as needed. After pouring the sauce over the lamb chops, serve immediately.

Notes:

- Lamb chops can be prepared by seasoning them with salt, pepper, thyme, and lemon zest and chilling them for up to an hour.
- Lamb chops can be stored for about 3 days. Keep leftovers in an airtight container in the refrigerator.

2. Lamb Roast

A leg of lamb is roasted in the oven with herbs and spices.

Carnivore Lamb Leg Roast

Ingredients:

- 1 tsp. salt
- 3 ½ lb. leg of lamb
- 1 tbsp. chopped fresh rosemary
- 2 tabs of melted fat or bacon grease
- 4 minced garlic cloves
- 1 tsp. pepper
- 1 tbsp. Chopped fresh thyme leaves

Instructions:

1. Allow the lamb to come to room temperature on the kitchen counter for two to three hours. You can ensure uniform cooking by doing so. The oven is preheated at 375°F (190°C).
2. In a small bowl, combine all of your chosen seasonings. Place the lamb in a roasting pan. Before pressing the spice mixture into the top side of the lamb, score it all over with a sharp knife. Alternately, make around 15 small slits all over the top of the lamb with a paring knife and insert seasonings into the incisions.
3. Roast the lamb for 30 minutes, fat side up, to brown and sear the outside. Once seared, remove and cover with foil, then put back in the oven.
4. Continue to roast for 45 minutes at 250°F (120°C). Transfer the lamb to a dish and set it aside for 15 minutes before slicing. Keep the fat and liquid in the roasting dish.
5. Using a large, sharp knife, slice the lamb roast while holding it steady on a carving fork. Always cut with the grain. Drizzle the fat and juice on top before serving.
6. The rare to medium-rare meat obtained by this approach tastes the best. Internal temperatures for rare and medium meats should be around 135°F (58°C) and 150°F (65°C), respectively.

3. Lamb Kofta

Ground lamb is spiced and shaped into meatballs or sausage-like shapes before being cooked. Lamb kofta is a Middle Eastern dish made of ground lamb, onion, garlic, and numerous spices shaped into patties, balls, or logs and grilled. The meal is commonly served skewered (kabob style) and unskewered, depending on the cooking process and option.

Ingredients:

- ½ tsp. salt
- 1 medium Spanish onion, minced
- 1 lb. lean ground lamb
- ¼ c. finely chopped curly parsley
- 1 clove of garlic, minced
- ¼ tsp. ground pepper
- ¼ tsp. allspice
- ¼ tsp. Cinnamon
- ⅛ tsp. ground cloves

Instructions:

1. Preheat the grill to medium-high heat. In a medium mixing bowl, knead the lamb with the onion, garlic, parsley, salt, pepper, cinnamon, allspice, and cloves until the ingredients are evenly distributed.
2. Divide the mixture into four equal pieces. Form each component into an 8-inch sausage. The meat is impaled on a strong metal skewer.
3. Lightly oil a folded paper towel. Hold the towel with tongs. Dredge the grill rack along the grates in your direction to grease it because the oil will soon cook off. You should do this straight away before adding the meat.
4. After 9 to 13 minutes of cooking time, flip the lamb kofta every 3 to 4 minutes. Allow the skewer to rest on a cutting surface for 4 minutes before slicing.

Notes:

- Flare-ups on the grill are probable if your lamb is not exceptionally lean. If this happens while grilling kofta on a gas grill, switch off one of the burners and set the skewers over the side of the grill that has been turned off. To prevent sticking, lubricate the grill.

4. Lamb Curry

Cubes of lamb are simmered in a spicy sauce.

Total Time: 1 hour 35 minutes

Ingredients:

- 500 g. Lamb
- 2 onions
- 1 tsp. Chili Powder
- 50 ml. Olive Oil
- 1 tsp. Ginger Paste
- 3 tomatoes
- 1 tsp. salt
- 1 tsp. garlic Paste
- 1 tsp. turmeric Powder Haldi
- 1 tsp. coriander Powder
- ½ tsp. gram Masala
- 500 ml. Water
- 1 tsp. dried Fenugreek Leaves Methi
- Coriander

Instructions:

1. Heat the olive oil in a skillet over medium heat until hot. Cook for 5 minutes or until the onions are soft.
2. Cook for 1 minute after adding the ginger and garlic paste. Cook for 5 minutes or until the tomatoes are soft.
3. Add salt, turmeric powder, chili powder, and coriander powder, and simmer the spices for 3-4 minutes.
4. Add water and simmer for 8 to 10 minutes after adding the spices to the lamb or mutton.
5. If the meat is still not done, add more water to help it cook for another 45 to 60 minutes. To keep the meat from burning, cover the pan with a lid.
6. Stir in the coriander, fenugreek, and gram masala. Enjoy!

5. Lamb Shank

A lamb shank is slow-cooked in a flavorful broth until tender.

Total Time: 3 hours 30 minutes

Ingredients:

- 1 tbsp. olive oil

- 4 lamb shanks
- 1 c. carrot, finely diced
- 1 onion finely diced
- ⅓ c. balsamic vinegar
- 4 cloves garlic minced
- 1 c. finely diced celery
- 2 bay leaves
- 3 tbsp. tomato paste
- ¼ tsp. pepper
- 3 c. beef stock
- ¼ tsp. salt
- 1 tsp. dried thyme

Instructions:

1. Preheat the oven to 350 degrees F. (175 degrees Celsius).
2. Season the lamb shank on all sides with salt and pepper. Sear the shanks on all sides in a large pan with oil over medium-high heat (approx. 8 minutes). After searing, place on a dish.
3. When the veggies soften, add the garlic, onion, celery, and carrot, and cook for 5 minutes.
4. After adding the balsamic vinegar, tomato paste, beef stock, thyme, bay leaves, salt, and pepper, stir everything together in the pan. Bring to a gentle boil. When the sauce has finished simmering, return the lamb shanks to the pan and spoon some sauce. Cook for 1 ½ hours in the oven with a cover on.

Seafood (Continuation)

1. Fried Shrimp

Whole shrimp are breaded and fried in hot oil until golden brown.

Prep Time: 15 minutes

Total Time: 19 minutes

Servings: 5

Ingredients:

- ½ c. flour
- 1 lb. shrimp peeled and deveined
- 1 tsp. onion powder
- 2 c. oil
- 1 tsp. paprika
- 1 tsp. garlic powder
- ½ tsp. salt
- 2 eggs, beaten
- ½ tsp. black pepper
- 1 c. panko breadcrumbs

Instructions:

1. Toss the shrimp with the salt and pepper in a medium bowl.
2. Add the flour, onion powder, garlic powder, paprika, salt, and pepper in a small bowl.
3. Place panko in a third bowl and eggs in a second.
4. Coat the shrimp in the flour mixture, the egg, and the panko crumbs. Arrange them on a tray or a flat dish.

5. The oil temperature in a deep skillet or deep frying pan should be around 375 degrees Fahrenheit. (190 degrees C).
6. Cook a few shrimp at a time in the hot oil until golden brown. 2 to 3 minutes, depending on the size of the shrimp.
7. Using a slotted spoon, remove the fried shrimp and place them on paper towels to drain.

Notes:

- Cook the shrimp in batches to avoid overcrowding the pot.
- As the coating thickens, it becomes crisper.
- Be careful not to overcook them. When overcooked, they become chewy and difficult to consume.

2. Lobster with Butter

A whole lobster is boiled and then served with melted butter.

Total Time: 25 minutes

Ingredients:

- 2 tbsp. water
- 1 ¾ lb. live lobster or 2 uncooked lobster tails
- 2 tomatoes cut into large chunks

- 1 clove of garlic, very finely minced
- ½ c. salted butter 1 stick, cut into 1 tablespoon chunks
- A few fresh basils leave chiffonade

Instructions:

Using Lobster Tails:

1. Cut the lobster's shell down its back using sharp kitchen shears. Turn the bottom shell over and chop it down. Remove the meat by peeling off the shell.

Using Whole Lobster:

1. Bring a large pot of water to a boil if you intend to use live, whole lobster. Turn off the heat and add the lobster. Cook with the cover on for three minutes. After removing the lobster meat from the shell, cut it into large chunks.
2. 1 tablespoon of water should be simmering on low heat in a saucepan. Add 1 tsp of butter and whisk. After the first batch of butter has melted, add more. Continue by adding each remaining piece of butter one at a time. Make sure the mixture does not boil to prevent the butter from separating.
3. Add the lobster pieces and simmer for 5 minutes on medium-low heat, turning about once per minute. Make sure the mixture does not boil. After extracting the lobster, divide it into two serving basins.
4. Add the garlic and raise the heat slightly in the same saucepan with the remaining butter. When the mixture smells good, add the tomatoes and cook for a few minutes or until some juices are released. Lightly smash the tomatoes to extract more juice. Then finish with the basil. Serve immediately with tomatoes on top of the lobster.

3. Grilled Fish

A piece of fish is marinated and then grilled until cooked through.

Ingredients:

- 1 tbsp. olive oil
- 3 slices of lemon
- 1 whole fish, gutted and scaled
- 1–2 tsp. kosher salt
- 1 small bunch of fresh parsley
- Spray oil

Instructions:

1. Prepare a grill with off-center coals for two-zone grilling. As a result, a hot and cool zone for cooking is formed. Around 400°F should be considered hot.
2. Pat the fish dry from the cavity to the skin with a paper towel. Fill the cavity with lemon and parsley after applying salt.
3. Drizzle the olive oil over the outside of the fish, coating both sides completely. Season both sides liberally with salt.

4. Spray some oil on the hot side of the grill grates, but not too close. Place the fish onto the greased grates over the hot embers to sear and crisp the skin.
5. You will now turn the fish over while it is still cooking. Spray a separate section of the grates over the hot coals where you want to flip the fish, then use a fish spatula or stiff spatula to carefully flip it over. Cook for 2 minutes.
6. If your fish becomes excessively browned, move it to the intermediate region (halfway between the hot and cool zones) to cook it more slowly.
7. If you haven't achieved the desired char/color on the outside, repeat the high-heat searing process of spraying and flipping; this time, add spray oil to the fish's surface. Spray directly into the skin that is facing up just before flipping.
8. Once the fish has reached an acceptable color, move the fish to the indirect side to finish cooking. Spray the grill grates where you intend to move the fish with nonstick cooking spray.
9. Keep an eye on the meat as it changes from transparent to opaque to determine when the fish is done. The fish is done for a more precise reading when a thermometer reads 140 degrees.
10. When finished, serve immediately, and don't forget to appreciate that succulent cheek meat bite!

4. Seafood Paella

A traditional Spanish dish made with rice, seafood, and vegetables.

Total Time: 65 minutes

Servings: 6 servings

Ingredients:

- ¼ tsp. salt

- 4 ½ c. chicken stock
- ½ yellow onion
- 3 tbsp. olive oil
- ½ tsp. saffron threads
- ½ red bell pepper
- 6 oz. mild dried chorizo sausage
- 14 oz. fire-roasted diced tomatoes
- 3 cloves garlic
- 3 c. short-grain rice
- 1 lb. large shrimp
- 1 lb. littleneck clams,
- 1 c. frozen green peas
- 1 lb. mussels
- ¼ c. chopped parsley

Instructions:

1. Light a charcoal grill and let it burn until it is completely covered in gray ash (375°F for gas grills).
2. Bring the stock to a boil in a saucepan over medium heat to steep the saffron. Season with salt and saffron. Allow the saffron to steep for at least 15 minutes after turning off the heat. Taste and season with more salt if necessary.
3. Heat the oil in a 12- to 14-inch cast iron or stainless steel skillet over medium heat to prepare the soffit foundation. After adding the red pepper, cook for 5 to 7 minutes or until the onion is translucent. Stir in the chorizo and garlic.
4. Arrange the items near the grill. Place the pan with the sofrito, rice, tomatoes, infused stock, salt, peas, shrimp, mussels, and clams near the grill.

5. Place the skillet with the sofrito on the grill to cook the paella. Toss the rice often for 4 to 5 minutes or until gently toasted and coated with oil.
6. After mixing, add the stock, tomatoes, and peas. After seasoning, add more salt if desired.
7. Spread the rice evenly across the bottom of the pan. Cook the rice on the grill without stirring for 15 minutes or until the rice has absorbed the majority of the liquid. If the mixture appears dry without stirring, add about 1 cup of hot water.
8. Place the mussels and clams in the rice, hinge sides up, to allow the shell juices to seep into the rice. Form a circle with the shrimp and shellfish.
9. Cook the dish for another 6 to 10 minutes, depending on how hot your grill is, or until the mussels and clams are open and the rice is well cooked.

5. Clam Chowder

A creamy soup made with clams, potatoes, and onions.

Ingredients:

- 1 tsp. minced garlic
- 1 ½ tsp. kosher salt
- Chopped parsley to garnish

- 4 slices bacon, chopped
- ½ c, chopped onion
- 2 tbsp. butter
- 8 oz. bottle of clam juice
- ¼ tsp. ground black pepper
- 3 c. peeled and chopped celery root
- 16 oz. raw chopped clams
- 8 oz. mascarpone cheese
- 1 ½ c. water

Instructions:

1. Cook the bacon in a large saucepan over medium heat for 2 to 3 minutes or until it is lightly browned but not crispy.
2. Cook for 2 to 3 minutes until the onions are translucent and fragrant, with the celery root, onion, garlic, salt, and pepper.
3. Cover and cook on low heat for 15 to 20 minutes when the celery root is tender. Pour in the water and clam juice.
4. When you add the clams and stir, the mascarpone cheese should melt, and the broth should become creamy.
5. Simmer on low for 3 minutes or until the clams are slightly cooked. Never, ever boil.
6. Remove from the heat and stir in the butter, allowing it to melt.
7. Taste and add extra salt and pepper as needed.
8. Garnish with parsley and serve hot.

Game

1. *Grilled Rabbit*

A whole rabbit is marinated and grilled until fully cooked. This recipe is intended to be cooked on the grill because the flavor is fantastic, but it also roasts well at 200°C/400°F/gas. If you're cooking the rabbit pieces in the oven, turn them several times to ensure even coloring and cooking. If you want to cook it on the grill, you'll need five wooden or metal skewers.

Here are some general guidelines for roasting or grilling:

- Liver and Kidneys: 4 minutes
- Shoulder and Legs: 35-40 minutes
- Ribs and Saddle: 15-20 minutes
- Belly: 25-30 minutes

Ingredients:

- 4 cloves garlic peeled
- 1.2 kg rabbit, preferably wild, jointed
- 1 lemon, zest, and juice of
- Olive oil
- 1 tsp. honey
- 1 handful of fresh thyme and rosemary leaves picked
- 4 thick slices of higher-welfare pancetta
- Salt
- Freshly ground black pepper

Instructions:

1. Place the rabbit bits in a bowl. Using a mortar and pestle or a liquidizer, crush or blend the thyme and rosemary leaves to a pulp. Then, repeat the process with the garlic cloves. After mixing in 8 tablespoons of olive

oil, lemon zest, juice, and honey, pour this over the rabbit. Set the meat aside to come to room temperature while you start the grill.

2. Gather a few fresh thyme sprigs and tie them together to make a small brush. Each time you turn the meat, dab a little marinade onto it to create a flavor-coated layer.

3. Remove the meat from the marinade, season with salt and pepper, and set aside. Assemble the pancetta between the two pieces of the belly with three skewers. Preheat the grill for the shoulders and legs. After they've been cooking for 10 minutes, add the belly. After another ten minutes, add the saddle and ribs. Make sure to flip the meat over from time to time.

4. Maintain the temperature by basting it with the marinade regularly. Each kidney should be divided in half and opened like a book. 1 piece of liver (cut into four pieces), 1 kidney, and more liver should be on each remaining skewer.

5. When the meat is perfectly cooked, add the skewered chunks of kidney and liver to the grill and cook until golden, together with the two remaining slices of pancetta. After a few minutes, place the browned pancetta on top of the meat toward the cooler end of the grill. Gather everyone around the table now.

6. Serve the rabbit with white beans, roast potatoes, grilled vegetables, or salads, depending on your mood and the weather. Simply place the meat on a board and serve.

2. Venison Stew

Venison stew includes slices of venison simmered in a tomato and spice-based sauce until tender.

Ingredients:

- ¼ c. all-purpose flour
- 2 lb. venison stew meat (or moose, elk, beef, antelope, bear –any red meat)
- 2 tsp. salt, divided
- 1–2 tbsp. high heat-tolerant oil or fat (deer/ duck/ beef fat, clarified butter avocado oil)
- 1 tsp. pepper
- 3–4 large carrots, diced
- 1 lb. baby, gold potatoes, quartered
- 1 onion, diced
- 3 celery stalks, diced
- 2 tsp. Herbs de Provence
- 4–5 garlic cloves, minced
- 4 c. beef or venison stock
- 1 (15oz.) can of diced tomatoes, drained
- 5–10 dashes of Worcestershire sauce

- ½ c. red wine (dry red like a Cabernet or Bordeaux is lovely)
- Optional: 3 tbsp. corn starch, tapioca starch, or arrowroot powder,

Instructions:

1. Whisk together the flour, ½ teaspoon of pepper, and 1 teaspoon of salt in a larger mixing bowl. To remove any liquid, pat the venison dry thoroughly with a towel. Toss the venison chunks in the flour mixture again as soon as they are evenly coated.
2. Heat the oil or fat in a large skillet set over medium-high heat. When the pan is hot, sear the venison all over. Working in batches may be necessary to avoid crowding the meat.
3. After searing the meat and potatoes, place them in the bottom of a slow cooker.
4. Next, combine the tomatoes, stock, wine, Worcestershire sauce, Herbs de Provence, carrots, celery, onion, garlic, and the remaining 1 teaspoon salt and ½ teaspoon pepper in a large mixing bowl.
5. Set your slow cooker to low for 8 to 9 hours. Remove a few spoonfuls of the liquid after about 6 hours and pour them into a bowl or cup as an optional step for a thick stew. Stir constantly as the starch is added to form a slurry. After adding the slurry, thoroughly stir the stew and cover it with a lid to finish cooking.
6. Keep warm and serve with crusty bread!

Notes:

- Cook for 4-5 hours on high, but 8-9 hours on low is preferable. The meat will be softer, and the flavors will blend better.
- Because it's so lovely, seek out Herbs de Provence rather than substituting them.

3. Roast Duck

A whole duck is roasted in the oven with herbs and spices such as thyme, rosemary, parsley, and lemon.

Total Time: 2 hours 10 minutes

Servings: 4

Ingredients:

- 2 tbsp. olive oil
- 1 tbsp. garlic powder
- 5 lb. duck
- 1 tsp. Rosemary
- 1 tsp. thyme
- 1 tsp. sea salt
- 6 slices lemon for garnish
- 1 tsp. parsley
- 3 sprigs of fresh thyme and rosemary
- ½ lemon, juiced

Instructions:

1. Preheat the oven to 350 degrees Fahrenheit. Clean, dry, and salt the duck. Combine the olive oil, spices, and lemon juice to paste.
2. Spread the paste on the duck. Place the remainder of the squeezed lemon inside the duck's cavity.
3. In a roasting pan, combine the duck and ½ cup water.
4. Cook the duck for 120 minutes, basting every 30 minutes. It's done when the duck's fluids are clear and golden brown.
5. Remove from the oven and set aside for ten to fifteen minutes to cool. Serve immediately after slicing. Garnish with lemon slices, pan juices, and fresh thyme or rosemary.
6. Refrigerate in a glass dish for two days.

4. Pheasant Bake

A whole pheasant is baked in the oven with herbs and spices.

Ingredients:

- ¼ bunch of rosemary, divided use
- 1 pheasant
- ¼ bunch of sage, divided use
- 1 bunch of escarole
- 4 cloves of garlic, thinly sliced
- ¼ lb. white truffle butter melted
- 1 c. duck and veal demi-glace
- ¼ c. white wine or vermouth
- 10 Cipollini onions peeled

Instructions:

1. Preheat the oven to 400 degrees Fahrenheit. Choose each herb with a single leaf; remove any stems. Half of the herbs should be finely chopped and set aside.
2. Gently detach the pheasant skin from the breasts and thighs with your index finger to avoid tearing the skin. The full-leaf herbs should be applied piece by piece beneath the epidermis.
3. After being coated in softened truffle butter, the bird should have a shell-like exterior. Season with salt and pepper to taste.
4. Bake the bird for 10 minutes at 400 degrees, then reduce the heat to 350 degrees for another 30 minutes. Place the bird on top of the peeled cipollini onions in a skillet. While the bird roasts, sauté the escarole with the garlic and season with salt and pepper. You may need to add a little water if you want the escarole to be soft.
5. After deglazing the roasting pan with white wine or vermouth, add the demi-glace. Before reducing by half and straining, stir in the minced herbs and season with salt and pepper to taste.
6. Remove the breast meat from the pheasant (three lengthwise slices for each breast), then remove the thighs. Each plate should include a thigh and a layer of sliced breast meat. Serve with chilled white wine and a dollop of sauce on top.

5. Wild Boar Chops

Wild boar chops are grilled or pan-fried until cooked through.

Total Time: 6 hours 30 minutes

Total Servings: 4

Ingredients:

- 1 tbsp. Lawry's Seasoned Pepper
- 2 tsp Lawry's Seasoned Salt
- 2 lb. boar/pork chops
- 2 tbsp. minced fresh rosemary
- ⅓ cup olive oil
- 8 whole garlic cloves – (to 10)
- 1 lemon, juice only
- 1 c. carrots
- 6 whole peeled shallots – (to 8)
- 1 cup dry red wine
- 2 celery stalks cut 2" pieces
- ½ cup chilled butter cut into 4 pieces

Instructions:

1. Season the meat with Lawry's Seasoned Salt and Lawry's Seasoned Pepper. Seasoned chops are combined with ¼ cup olive oil, rosemary, and lemon juice. Refrigerate for 6 to 12 hours, covered.
2. Heat the remaining oil in a large oven-safe skillet. Chops are added and lightly browned on both sides. Remove and set aside the chops.
3. Sauté the carrots, celery, garlic, and shallots until they brown.
4. Return the chops to the pan and preheat the oven to 375°F. Cook for 5 to 8 minutes more or until the chops are done and the shallots are tender.
5. Keep the chops warm after removing them from the pan. Place the pan over medium-high heat and add the wine. Reduce the wine to about 2 teaspoons. After removing from the heat, whisk in the chilled butter until melted.
6. Arrange the chops on top of the vegetables on serving plates. Serve the sauce over the chops.

Snacks and Salads

1. French Fries

Potatoes are sliced and fried in hot oil until crispy.

Total Time: 30 minutes

Servings: 4

Ingredients:

- ⅓ c. white sugar
- 2 c. warm water
- 6 c. vegetable oil for frying
- 2 large russet potatoes, peeled and sliced into ¼-inch strips
- Salt to taste

Instructions:

1. Combine the heated water and sugar in a medium mixing bowl. Soak potatoes in a water mixture for 15 minutes. Remove the potatoes from the water and pat them dry with paper towels.
2. In a deep fryer, heat the oil to 375°F (190 degrees C).
3. Cook potatoes in hot oil for 5–6 minutes or until golden. Season with salt and pat dry with paper towels.

2. Chicken Salad

A salad with cubed chicken, vegetables, and a vintage

Total Time: 20 minutes

Servings: 4 servings

Ingredients:

For the Salad:

- 1 medium tomato, diced
- 1 head of baby romaine lettuce, diced
- 1 ½ c. diced cucumber
- 1 small red pepper, diced
- 1 ¼ lb. cooked chicken, diced

- ¼ c. diced red onion
- ⅓ c. Kalamata olives
- ½ c. crumbled feta

For the Dressing:

- ¼ c. red wine vinegar
- ¼ c. avocado or olive oil
- 2 cloves garlic, minced
- 1 tbsp. lemon juice
- ½ tsp. dried marjoram
- 2 tsp. Dijon mustard
- Salt and pepper to taste

Instructions:

For the Salad:

- Option 1: Arrange all ingredients in decorative lines on a large dish. Allow guests to take as many servings as they like.
- Option 2: Combine all ingredients in a large mixing bowl and divide them evenly among four large plates.

For the Dressing:

- Shake all the dressing ingredients thoroughly in a jar or bottle with a sealable top. Serve alongside the salad.

3. Chicken Salad

A salad with cubed chicken, vegetables, and a vinaigrette dressing.

Ingredients:

- 7 tbsp. reduced-fat balsamic vinaigrette dressing
- 1 lb. uncooked thin sliced chicken breasts
- 1 medium red onion cut into ¼-inch slices
- 1 medium zucchini (8 oz), cut lengthwise in half
- 6 c. torn arugula
- 4 plum (Roma) tomatoes, cut in half
- ½ c. crumbled feta cheese (2 oz)

Instructions:

1. Preheat a gas or charcoal grill. Brush 1 tablespoon of the dressing over the chicken. Brush the grill rack gently. Over medium heat, grill the chicken, zucchini, and onion. Cook, flipping once, for 8 to 10 minutes, or until the chicken is no longer pink in the center and the vegetables are soft. For the last 4 minutes of cooking, grill the tomato halves.

2. Remove the chicken and vegetables from the grill and place them on a cutting board. Cut the chicken into thin crosswise slices, and roughly chop the vegetables.

3. Combine the chicken, vegetables, and the remaining 6 tablespoons of dressing in a large mixing bowl. Combine the arugula and cheese in a mixing bowl. Serve immediately.

4. Caesar Salad

A salad with romaine lettuce, croutons, Parmesan cheese, and a Caesar dressing.

Total Time: 30 minutes

Servings: 4 to 6

Ingredients:

- 4 cloves of garlic, minced
- ½ c. high-quality extra virgin olive oil, including more for brushing
- ¼ c. fresh lemon juice
- 1 baguette, preferably a day old, thinly sliced
- 4 oz. Parmesan cheese, grated
- 2 large eggs
- 1 tsp. anchovy paste, or 1 to 2 anchovies, minced
- ½ tsp. kosher salt (or to taste)
- 4 to 6 small heads of romaine lettuce, rinsed, patted dry, wilted outer leaves discarded
- ¼ tsp. Freshly ground black pepper (or to taste)

Instructions:

1. Combine ½ cup olive oil and garlic in a large mixing bowl. Allow at least 30 minutes for your stay.

2. While the garlic sits, make the croutons. Lay out the baguette slices on a baking sheet. This might have to be done in batches.

3. Brush or spray melted butter with olive oil. If you want garlicky croutons, dip a pastry brush in the garlic-infused oil you made in the previous step.

4. Broil the tops for 1-2 minutes or until lightly browned. Don't walk away because these can quickly turn brown to charred. Set aside to cool after removing from the oven.

5. To the oil-garlic mixture, add the minced anchovies or anchovy paste, as well as the eggs. Whisk until completely smooth. Squeeze in ¼ cup lemon juice after seasoning with salt and pepper. Half of the Parmesan cheese should be included. Season with additional lemon juice, salt, and pepper to taste. The lemon should give the dressing a tang without overpowering it.

6. Remove romaine lettuce chunks with your hands: Remove romaine lettuce chunks with your hands rather than with a knife. Toss the salad in the dressing until evenly coated. Toss with the rest of the Parmesan cheese.

7. To serve, coarsely chop the toasted bread and toss it with the salad. Brush in any crumbs left over from the bread-chopping process. Toss and serve immediately.

5. *Steak Salad*

A salad with grilled steak, vegetables, and a vinaigrette dressing.

Total Time: 45 minutes

Servings: 4 servings

Ingredients:

- ¼ c. balsamic vinegar
- ½ tsp. kosher salt
- ¼ tsp. black pepper
- 2 tsp. Dijon mustard
- ½ c. extra-virgin olive oil
- 1 tsp. mayonnaise, optional
- Kosher salt for seasoning
- 1 lb. flank steak or flat iron steak
- 2 tbsp. olive oil
- Black pepper, for seasoning
- 4 c. romaine lettuce
- 4 c. arugula, 1-inch pieces
- 1 c. cherry tomatoes, cut in half
- 2 c. radicchio, 1-inch pieces

- ¼ c. thinly sliced radish
- ½ c. thinly sliced cucumber
- ¼ c. feta cheese
- 1 medium avocado, sliced or diced
- ¼ c. diced red onion

Equipment:

- Instant-Read Thermometer
- Cast Iron Skillet
- Steak Salad

Instructions:

1. Whisk together the vinegar, mustard, mayonnaise, salt, and pepper in a medium mixing bowl. Gently whisk in the olive oil until the dressing thickens and emulsifies.
2. Pat the meat dry with paper towels. Season both sides with salt and pepper.
3. Preheat a large cast-iron skillet over high heat. When the oil is hot, add the steak and press it down. Cook for 4 minutes or until the top is browned.
4. Cook for 3 to 5 minutes, or until the steak reaches an internal temperature of 120 to 125°F (49 to 52°C) for medium-rare.
5. Set the steak aside on a cutting board for 10 minutes. Cut the meat into 14-inch thick pieces perpendicular to the grain. Make it smaller if desired.
6. Combine the arugula, romaine, and radicchio in a large serving bowl. Add tomatoes, cucumber, radish, onion, sirloin, avocado, and feta cheese to the salad. Drizzle the balsamic vinaigrette over the steak salad.

6. BLT Sandwich

A sandwich made with bacon, lettuce, tomato, and mayonnaise.

Total Time: 20 minutes

Servings: 1

Ingredients:

- 2 slices of high-quality sandwich bread,
- 1 c. finely shredded iceberg lettuce
- Freshly ground black pepper
- 3 strips of thick-cut, naturally cured bacon
- 2 to 4 thick slices of ripe tomato
- Coarse sea salts
- 2 tbsp. mayonnaise

Special Equipment: A griddle or large cast iron skillet, a bacon press, or a masonry trowel are all useful tools.

Instructions:

1. In a griddle or skillet over medium-low heat, melt the butter. To keep the bacon flat as it cooks, place it on top of a bacon press, skillet, or masonry trowel. Cook until the first side of the bacon is lightly

browned, about 5 minutes, then flip, cover, and cook until the bacon is browned on both sides and the fat has rendered. Place the bacon on a platter lined with paper towels and set aside.

2. Toast the bread in the bacon fat over medium-low heat, stirring occasionally, until both sides are evenly brown.
3. On a work surface, spread mayonnaise on both top faces of toasted bread. Divide the lettuce between the two slices of bread. Season tomato slices with coarse salt and freshly ground pepper to taste on 1 piece of bread.
4. Cut the bacon slices in half and stack them in two layers of three half slices each on the sandwich, switching the orientation of the bacon in each layer for structural stability. Close the sandwich and cut it in half diagonally. Serve immediately.

6. Hot Dogs

A frankfurter sausage served in a hot dog bun, often with toppings such as ketchup, mustard, and onions.

Ingredients:

- 1 c. all-purpose flour
- ¼ tsp. salt
- 1 c. yellow cornmeal
- ¼ c. granulated sugar
- 1 qt. vegetable oil
- ¼ tsp. black pepper
- 4 tsp. baking powder
- 2 packages of frankfurters
- 1 egg
- 1 c. milk

- 16 wooden skewers or popsicle sticks

Instructions:

1. Combine cornmeal, flour, salt, pepper, sugar, and baking powder in a medium mixing bowl. Mix in the eggs and milk until well combined.
2. In a large frying pan over medium heat, heat the oil. Insert the frankfurters with wooden skewers. Dip the frankfurters into the batter and coat evenly.
3. Fry 2 or 3 corn dogs until golden brown, about 3 minutes. Using paper towels, pat dry.

7. Buffalo Wings

Chicken wings are breaded and fried, then coated in a spicy sauce.

Ingredients:

- 1 ½ c. water
- 3 tbsp. cornstarch
- 1 c. flour
- 2 lb. chicken wing segments
- Vegetable oil for frying
- ⅔ c. gochujang sauce

- 1 tbsp. hardcore Carnivore Amplify (optional)
- 2 tbsp. rice vinegar
- ¼ c. soy sauce

Instructions:

1. In a deep fryer or large heavy-bottomed saucepan, heat the oil to 375°F. Place a sheet pan lined with paper towels on a wire rack.
2. In a mixing bowl, combine the flour, cornstarch, and water. Using a whisk, thoroughly combine all ingredients.
3. Dip a wing into the batter with tongs, then remove and place in the hot oil, allowing excess batter to drip off. Repeat with the opposite wing half. You may need to do this in three batches if you have a small fryer or pot. After 7 minutes, remove the wings to a cooling rack to cool. Continue with the rest of the wings, ensuring the oil has cooled to room temperature between batches.
4. Place the wings back in the oil and fry for another 5 minutes or until they are a deep golden brown. Set aside at least 2-3 minutes after returning to the rack.
5. Combine the gochujang, soy sauce, and vinegar in a large mixing bowl while the wings cool. Whisk everything together to make a sauce. To coat the wings, toss them in the sauce in the basin. Serve immediately.

8. Pulled Pork Sandwich

Shredded pork is cooked with BBQ sauce and served on a bun.

Ingredients:

- 1 (4 lb.) pork shoulder roast
- 1 tsp. vegetable oil
- ½ c. apple cider vinegar
- 1 c. barbeque sauce

- ½ c. chicken broth
- 1 tbsp. prepared yellow mustard
- ¼ c. light brown sugar
- 1 tbsp. Worcestershire sauce
- 1 extra large onion, chopped
- 1 ½ tsp. dried thyme
- 1 tbsp. chili powder
- 2 large cloves of garlic, crushed
- 2 tbsp. butter, or as need
- 8 hamburger buns, split

Equipment: Slow cooker

Instructions:

1. Fill the slow cooker halfway with vegetable oil. Pour the pork roast, barbecue sauce, vinegar, and chicken broth into the slow cooker. Add brown sugar, yellow mustard, Worcestershire sauce, chili powder, onion, garlic, and thyme. Cook on low for 10 to 12 hours or high for 5 to 6 hours or until pork shreds easily with a fork.
2. Using two forks, shred the pork from the slow cooker. Return the shredded pork to the slow cooker, along with the liquids.
3. Spread butter inside both hamburger bun halves. Heat the buns in a skillet, butter side down, until golden brown. Put pulled pork on toasted buns.

Hopefully, these recipes will be useful when planning your daily meal on the carnivore diet.

Chapter 7: Meal Planning and Preparation Tips

How to Plan and Prepare Dinners for the Week

Your "knife skills" will be useless if you don't have a plan.

Reputable chefs thrive on multiple levels of menu planning, meticulous ingredient ordering, and the most efficient use of labor. Cooks prepare sauces, chop vegetables, and cook food that will be ready for serving at the end of the day.

If you want to eat healthier, meal preparation is essential. By stocking your pantry and refrigerator with items that support your strategy, you will set yourself up for success.

Most customers go to the store to buy the same items repeatedly. If you want to eat healthier or spend less money on prepared foods, you should plan.

Make Provisions for Flexibility

Cooking for oneself can allow you to do things your way. Do you prefer to keep it loose, or do you prefer to stick to a recipe? If you're new to meal planning, prepare the basics for three or four meals.

Doing the Math

Examine your weekly schedule. How many days are you going to be home for breakfast? Why not try all seven? Make a mental note of that number. Pick a day to cook. Do you have four hours on Saturday available? You should be able to get your essentials, a sauce, a dressing, and possibly a dessert.

The Groundwork: Create a Pantry

To help you plan your meals, you can do some improvising in your pantry. Sauces can be made during the meal preparation process or purchased and stored. You can also use frozen vegetables instead of preparing them on prep day.

- Canned salmon and tuna are ideal for a quick lunch or dinner.
- Pesto, salad dressings, curry pastes and simmer sauces, salsa, soy sauce, Asian marinades, and spicy sauce are all great to keep on hand.
- Stock up on your family's favorite frozen vegetables because they are already cooked.
- As a treat, serve frozen tortellini or ravioli. Cook and combine with cooked meats and vegetables, as well as canned sauce.
- Hard cheeses like Parmesan or Cheddar keep well and only need to be sprinkled on pasta or vegetables.

- Meat, seafood, beans, and tofu are examples of protein preps.
- White rice, quinoa, and bulgur all take 15 minutes to cook.
- Soups can be made quickly using boxed stocks and pre-cut meats and vegetables.

Plan to prepare protein portions for four meals—the simplest method is to roast chicken, beef, fish, or sliced, marinated tofu in the oven, then divide it among four containers.

Your Fundamental Preparation

Depending on what is being cooked, boil or bake them to make a quick salad, reheat them in a curry sauce, or microwave them on prep day.

Your primary preparation will be vegetables.

Vegetables: Roasted, par-cooked, and chopped vegetables for stir-frying or steaming.

Preheat the oven to roast your meats and a pan or two of your favorite roasted vegetables for the week in the winter. Caramelized Brussels sprouts, carrots, cauliflower, and other favorites can be stored and reheated for up to a week in the oven.

In the summer, you can simply chop your vegetables and store them in zip-top bags to steam, stir fry, or eat raw.

Salads and dressings form the basis of your meal preparation.

Salad greens should be made or purchased for each meal. Pre-washed greens are available in 4-5 ounce packs, which is enough for four side salads.

Making salad dressings saves money and gives you more control over the ingredients. This can be as simple as shaking olive oil, vinegar, and crushed garlic in a jar or as complex as making a creamy yogurt or tahini dressing to last the week. You'll be more likely to eat your salad with a tasty dressing.

How to Cook Perfectly Grilled Steak

You can dress up your meal, prep salads, or make a nice evening supper with this quick and easy dish. The thinner the steak, the faster it will reach the ideal medium rare temperature.

This is the solution if your steaks are constantly sticking to the grill!

Keep the spices simple for a good steak. Salt and pepper are always required. For a little extra flavor, add some fresh rosemary to the mix.

You can easily omit the butter, but the melted butter at the end is believed to add moisture to the steak. Allow it to sit on the steaks while they rest.

Warm Up the Grill

Turn on your grill and allow it to heat up to medium-high. You can use a gas or charcoal grill for cooking. Reduce the heat to medium for the steaks and place them on the grill. Set them at an angle to get the best char marks.

Steaks Should Be Oiled

Brush both sides of the steaks with olive oil. This keeps the steaks from sticking to the grill and ruining the lovely char!

Season the Steaks

Season the steaks with salt, pepper, and fresh rosemary.

Examine the Temperature

Grill the steaks for 4 minutes per side until the internal temperature reaches 130°F/55°C for a medium-rare steak.

Finish with Butter

When the steaks are done, place them on a plate and top them with a pat of butter. Wrap the platter in foil and set aside the steaks to rest while the butter melts.

Clean the Grill

The first step toward a perfectly cooked steak is to clean the grates! This lets you turn your steaks more easily and eliminates the burned flavor. Flipping will be much easier if the grates are oiled.

Let the Steaks Come to Room Temperature

This may seem risky, but it allows the steaks to cook faster in the center! Set your steaks on the counter for about 30 minutes while you prepare your supper.

Increase the Taste

This quick and easy steak recipe yields wonderfully juicy and tasty results every time. Try a marinade or more garlic and herbs to add extra taste!

Steak Doneness Chart

Steak temperatures to aim for:
- Rare: 120-130 °F or 49-54 °C
- Medium Rare: 130-135 °F or 54-57 °C

- Medium: 135-145 °F or 57-63 °C
- Medium Well: 145-155 °F or 63-68 °C
- Well Done: 155 °F plus or 68 °C plus

For safety, the USDA advises cooking steaks to at least 145 °F.

Tips for Cooking and Serving Chicken Breasts

Have a Good Understanding of the Chicken Breast

Boneless chicken breasts are more popular than bone-in chicken breasts and thighs because they cook faster. They are frequently found skinless, making them slimmer than their bone-in cousin, usually seen with the skin on. Of course, boneless chicken breasts are delicious by themselves. However, recipes containing chicken bits or shreds, such as salads, stews, soups, or casseroles, are preferable. That's not to say you can't cook a bone-in chicken breast and cut around the bone afterward.

The main advantage of bone-in chicken breasts is that the flesh is juicier and tender. The rib bone is kept connected, which aids in the uniform transfer of heat and the production of the desired soft meat. This is why it is more likely to appear on the menu of a fine dining establishment. Because of the fatty skin, bone-in chicken breasts are less lean than boneless, but the skin adds flavor and seals moisture in the bone-in option—think of it as a protective barrier. They are also less expensive than boneless chicken breasts, which must be processed more thoroughly. Bone-in chicken breasts, which can be served whole or chopped, are an excellent choice for taking center stage.

Easiest Ways to Cook Chicken Breasts—Including Grilled, Fried, and More

Chicken dinner, chicken meat! There's a reason it has a catchphrase. Chicken is easy to prepare and cook, and chicken breasts are a popular choice in many kitchens because they cook quickly and are lean. Chicken breasts are versatile and can be dressed up or down for a dinner party or a weekday meal.

They're ideal for meal prep and pre-packaged lunches. When cooked properly, chicken breasts are juicy and succulent. The disadvantage is that overcooking may cause them to dry out quickly, but if you're careful, cooking chicken breasts at home will yield excellent results every time.

Poach Chicken Breasts

Cooking the breasts gently in barely simmering water with a few seasonings keeps the flesh moist and soft without adding fat. Add sliced lemon, carrot, and celery slices, or half a yellow onion to boost the flavor. Both bone-in and boneless options are acceptable.

Grill Chicken Breasts

The key to tender grilled chicken breasts is to pound them to an even thickness. Begin with boneless, skinless chicken breasts, and you'll be done soon. Ideal for summer cookouts or a quick weeknight meal.

Fry Chicken Breasts

The only way to fry delicious chicken breasts is to coat them in seasoned breadcrumbs. Serve them on their own with a squeeze of lemon, on top of a salad, or as the foundation for a filling sandwich or chicken Parmesan. The oil temperature should be between 350 and 360°F if you have a deep-fry thermometer.

Chapter 8: Meal Plans and Menus for the Carnivore Diet

30-Day Carnivore Diet Sample Meal Plans

Week 1

| Day | Breakfast | Lunch | Dinner |

Monday	Grilled Ribeye Steak (8 Oz.)	Slow Roast Topside Of Beef (12 Oz.)	Slow Roast Topside Of Beef (12 Oz.)
Tuesday	Grilled Ground Beef Burger Patty (8 Oz.)	Bbq Beef Ribs (24 Oz.)	Bbq Sirloin Steak (12 Oz.)
Wednesday	Grilled Ground Beef Burger Patty (8 Oz.)	Bbq Beef Ribs (24 Oz.)	Bbq Sirloin Steak (12 Oz.)
Thursday	Grilled Ground Beef Burger Patty (8 Oz.)	Bbq Ground Beef Burger Patty	Bbq Beef Ribs (24 Oz.)
Friday	Grilled Ground Beef Burger Patty (8 Oz.) Slow-Cooked Beef	Bbq Ribeye Steak (12 Oz.)	Grilled Porterhouse Steak (12 Oz.)
Saturday	Grilled Sirloin Steak (8 Oz.)	Bbq Ribeye Steak (12 Oz.)	Bbq Beef Ribs (24 Oz.)
Sunday	Grilled Ground Beef Burger Patty (8 Oz.)	Patty (8 Oz.) Roasted Beef	Bbq Beef Ribs (24 Oz.)

Week 2

Day	Breakfast	Lunch	Dinner
Monday	2 Grilled Chicken Breasts With 4 Pork Chops Fried Or Grilled	Grilled Trout Fillets (16 Oz.)	Slow Roast Topside Of Beef (12 Oz.)
Tuesday	3 Sausages (5 Oz.)	Roasted Pork Belly (10 Oz.)	Slow Roast Topside Of Beef (12 Oz.)
Wednesday	2 Grilled Chicken Breasts	2 Grilled Chicken Breasts With 4pork Chops-Fried Or Grilled	"Slow Roast Topside Of Beef (12 Oz.)
Thursday	Grilled Ground Beef Burger Patty (8 Oz.) With Cheese	The Bone (15 Oz.) With Butter	Slow Roast Topside Of Beef (12 Oz.)

Friday	2 Grilled Chicken Breasts	Roast Salmon Cutlets (15 Oz.) With Butter	Grilled Ribeye Steak (12 Oz.)
Saturday	Grilled Pork Sausages (5 Oz.)	2 Grilled Chicken Breasts With 4 pork Chops Fried Or Grilled	Slow Roast Topside Of Beef (12 Oz.)
Sunday	Grilled Ground Beef Burger Patty (8 Oz.) With Cheese	Roasted Pork Belly (10 Oz.)	Grilled Ribeye Steak (12 Oz.)

Week 3

Day	Breakfast	Lunch	Dinner
Monday	Grilled Ribeye steak (8 Oz)	3 Grilled Chicken Breasts	Grilled Ribeye Steak (8 Oz.) Roasted Beef Liver (4 Oz.)
Tuesday	5 Slices Of Bacon (4 Oz.)	Roast Salmon Cutlets On The Bone (15 Oz.)	Grilled Ground Beefburger

	1-2 100% Pork Sausages (3 Oz.)		
Wednesday	Grilled Sirloin Steak (8 Oz.)	Roast Salmon Cutlets On The Bone (15 Oz.)	4 pork Chops Fried Or Grilled
Thursday	2 Grilled Chicken Breasts With Slow Roast Topside Of Beef (12 Oz.)	Roast Salmon Cutlets	Grilled Ribeye Steak (8 Oz.) Roasted Beef Liver (4 Oz.)
Friday	Grilled Ribeye Steak (12 Oz.)	Slow Roast Topside Of Beef (12 Oz.)	Grilled Ground Beefburger
Saturday	5 Slices Of Bacon (4 Oz.) 1-2 100% Pork Sausages (3 Oz.)	Roast Salmon Cutlets On The Bone (15 Oz.)	4 Fresh Lamb Chops (12 Oz.)
Sunday	Grilled Sirloin Steak (8 Oz.)	Roast Salmon Cutlets On The Bone (15 Oz.)	Grilled Sirloin Steak (12 Oz.)

Week 4

Day	Breakfast	Lunch	Dinner
Monday	Grilled Ground Beefburger	Grilled Ground Beef Burger Patty (12 Oz.)	4 pork Chops Fried Or Grilled (12 Oz.)
Tuesday	Grilled Beef (Grounded)Burger	Grilled Ribeye Steak (8 Oz.)	4 pork Chops Fried Or Grilled (12 Oz.)
Wednesday	Grilled Ribeye Steak (8 Oz.)	Grilled Ground Beef Burger Patty (12 Oz.)	Fatty Fish Cutlets On The Bone (15 Oz.)
Thursday	Grilled Ribeye Steak (8 Oz.)	Grilled Ground Beef Burger Patty (12 Oz.)	Slow Roast Topside Of Beef (12 Oz.)
Friday	Grilled Beef (Grounded) Burger	Grilled Ground Beef Burger Patty (12 Oz.)	Grilled Porterhouse Steak (12 Oz.)

Saturday	Grilled Ribeye Steak (8 Oz.)	Roasted Beefliver (4 Oz.)	Grilled Porterhouse Steak (12 Oz.)
Sunday	Grilled Ribeye Steak (8 Oz.)	Grilled Ribeye Steak (8 Oz.)	Slow Roast topside of Beef Kidney (4 Oz.)

Menu Suggestions for Different Occasions

Birthday Menu

- Carnivore cake
- Carnivore Club Sandwich

- Carnivore Pizza
- Pork Belly Chips
- Carnivore Sandwich Bread
- Carnivore Tortillas
- Carnivore Baguettes
- Crunchy Beef Bars
- Carnivore Beef Liver Pancakes
- Carnivore Beef Liver Waffles
- Easy Instant Pot Oxtails

Thanksgiving Menu

- Animal-Based Dinner Rolls (with Carnivore Option)
- Creamy Mashed Kabocha Squash
- Carnivore Gravy
- 3-Ingredient Cranberry Sauce
- Sweet Potato Casserole (without the Sweet Potato)
- Carnivore Mac & Cheese
- Butternut Squash Dip with Carnivore Crisps
- Pork Belly Chips with Honey Mustard Dipping Sauce
- Bacon-Wrapped Dates Stuffed with Raw Cheese

Christmas Menu

- Chicken Livers Peri-Peri
- Chicken Yakitori
- Pork Sausage
- Pork Spare Ribs
- Venison Meat Balls
- Venison Sausage

- Venison Samoosas

Romantic Dinner Menu

- Pap & Shebo Sauce
- Baked Potato
- Assorted Venison Sausages
- Venison Meatballs
- Chicken Livers Peri-Peri
- Pork Sausage
- Chicken Yakitori
- Rump Steak of Beef
- Pork
- Crocodile

Customized Meal Plans for Special Dietary Needs

Meal Plan for Lowering Cholesterol and Balancing Saturated Fats

Learn how to lower your high cholesterol and improve your heart health by following this simple 3-day low-cholesterol meal plan for beginners.

Day 1

Breakfast - 280 calories

- 1 serving of Cinnamon Roll Overnight Oats
- 1 5-oz. container of nonfat plain Greek yogurt

Breakfast Snack - 206 calories

- ¼ cup of unsalted dry-roasted almonds

Lunch - 428 calories

- 1 clementine
- Kale and Chicken Salad along with Peanut Dressing
- 1 serving of Sweet Potato

Lunch Snack - 112 calories

- ¼ cup hummus
- ½ cup cucumber, sliced

Dinner - 472 calories

- 1 serving of Stuffed Sweet Potato along with Hummus Dressing

Daily Totals: 85 g protein, 1,497 calories, 184 g carbohydrates, 52g fat, 42g fiber, 1,664mg sodium, 7g saturated fat

To acquire 1,200 calories, substitute ½ cup of sliced bell pepper for the breakfast snack and leave out the hummus for the noon snack.

To get to 2,000 calories, do the following: 1 large apple for breakfast, 1 large pear for breakfast snack, 1 cup nonfat, regular Greek yogurt for lunch, and 1 serve Guacamole Chopped Salad for supper.

Day 2

Breakfast - 280 calories

- 1 serving of Cinnamon Roll Overnight Oats
- 1 5-oz. container of nonfat plain Greek yogurt

Breakfast Snack - 131 calories

- 1 large pear

Lunch - 428 calories

- 1 clementine
- 1 serving of Sweet Potato, Kale, and Chicken Salad Plus Peanut Dressing

Lunch Snack - 197 calories

- ¼ cup raspberries
- 1 cup nonfat plain Greek yogurt
- 1 Tbsp. chopped walnuts

Dinner - 450 calories

- 1 serving of Turkey and Sweet Potato Chili
- 1 serving of Guacamole Chopped Salad

Daily Totals: 96 g protein, 1,486 calories, 33g fiber, 158g carbohydrates, 1,623 mg sodium, 57g fat, 9 g saturated fat

To acquire 1,200 calories, modify the breakfast snack to one plum and leave out the yogurt and chopped walnuts at lunch.

To get to 2,000 calories, do three tablespoons of chopped walnuts for the morning, ⅓ cup unsalted dry-roasted almonds for breakfast snack, and a 1-ounce slice of whole-wheat bread for supper.

Day 3

Breakfast - 293 calories

- 1 serving of Apple & Peanut Butter Toast

Snack - 131 calories

- 1 large pear

Lunch - 387 calories

- 1 medium orange
- 1 serving Veggie and Hummus Sandwich

Snack - 206 calories

- ¼ cup of unsalted dry-roasted almonds

Dinner - 504 calories

- 1 serving Sheet-Pan Salmon along with Sweet Potatoes & Broccoli

Daily Totals: 1,521 calories, 153g carbohydrates, 67 g protein, 37 g fiber, 12 g saturated fat, 76g fat, 1,257 mg sodium

To acquire 1,200 calories, modify the breakfast snack to 1 clementine, leave out the orange at lunch, and replace it with 1 plum.

To consume 2,000 calories: Add ⅓ of walnut halves to breakfast. Lunch should include 1 cup of nonfat plain Greek yogurt and 1 big apple as a snack.

Vegetarian and Vegan Meal Plans

Vegan Diet Fundamentals and How to Begin

A vegan diet is a plant-based diet that excludes all animal products, including meat, fish, dairy, and honey. The vegetarian diet excludes meat and fish but allows for dairy and eggs.

To reap the benefits of this eating plan, focus on nutrient-dense whole foods like beans, lentils, nuts, seeds, whole grains, and plenty of fruits and vegetables.

Try to incorporate protein foods such as peanut butter, beans, lentils, tofu, seitan, and pecans into the majority of your meals to keep you satisfied between meals. If the vegan diet seems overwhelming, start with a couple of meatless days per week and work your way up.

What Can Be Eaten on a Vegan Diet

- Edamame
- Beans
- Tofu
- Lentils
- Soy
- Whole grains (oatmeal, quinoa, brown rice, wheat bread)

- Nuts, seeds, and nut kinds of butter
- Seitan
- Fruits
- Avocado
- Tempeh
- Vegetables
- Coconut
- Olives and olive oil
- Nutritional Yeast

Sample Meal Plan

Here's a one-week meal plan that includes some healthful items that may be eaten on a vegan diet.

Day	Breakfast	Lunch	Dinner	Snacks
Monday	Potato Toast Spiced With Peanut Butter & Banana	Tempeh Taco Salad With Quinoa, Avocados, Beans, Onions, Tomatoes, And Cilantro	Oat Risotto With Swiss Chard, Mushrooms, And Butternut Squash	Vegan Protein Shake, Mixed Berries, And Walnuts

Tuesday	Broccoli, Tomatoes, Eggless Quiche With Silken Tofu, And Spinach	Chickpea & Spinach Curry With Brown Rice	Olives, Peppers, Mediterranean Lentil Salad With Cucumbers, Sun-Dried Tomatoes, Kale, And Parsley	Sliced Pear, Chia Seeds, Roasted Edamame, And Energy Balls Made From Oats, Nut Butter, And Dried Fruit
Wednesday	Avocado, Tempeh Bacon With Sautéed Mushrooms And Wilted Arugula	A Side Salad And Whole-Grain Pasta With Lentil "Meatballs"	Cauliflower And Chickpea Tacos, Along With Guacamole And Pico De Gallo	Kale Chips, Trail Mix, And Air-Popped Popcorn
Thursday	Coconut Yogurt With Berries, Walnuts, And Chia Seeds	Herbed Couscous, Baked Tofu With Sautéed Red Cabbage	Mushroom Lentil Loaf With Garlic Cauliflower And Italian Green Beans	Seaweed Crisps, Bell Peppers With Guacamole, Fruit Leather
Friday	Oats With Apple Slices, Pumpkin Seeds, Cinnamon, And Nut Butter	Black Bean Veggie Burger Along With Steamed Broccoli & Sweet Potato Wedges	Collard Greens, Mac And "Cheese" Along With Nutritional Yeast	Coconut Chia Pudding And Granola, Pistachios
Saturday	Whole-Grain Toast And Nutritional Yeast Alongside A Vegan Protein Shake	Baked Potato And Lentil Chili With Grilled Asparagus	Tomatoes, Onions, Vegetable Paella With Brown Rice, Artichoke, And Chickpeas	Almonds, Fruit Salad, And Carrots With Hummus
Sunday	Tomatoes, Breakfast Skillet With Tempeh,	Garlic-Ginger Tofu Along With Stir-	Corn, And Bean Salad, Bell Peppers,	Frozen Grapes, And Celery, Along

| | Broccoli, Kale, And Zucchini | Fried Veggies And Quinoa | Tomatoes, And Onions | With Almond Butter |

Chapter 9: FAQs about the Carnivore Diet and Lifestyle

1. What Can Be Eaten on The Carnivore Diet?

Beef, chicken, pork, lamb, bison, turkey, and other seafood are examples of meats that can be eaten on the carnivore diet. Other animal products include eggs, lard, bone marrow, bone broth, fat, cheese, and milk.

2. Is the Carnivore Diet Safe?

The carnivore diet is safe; many societies worldwide eat only meat yearly.

3. Can You Lose Weight on the Carnivore Diet?

Many people lose weight after starting a carnivorous diet. You may notice changes in your weight, appetite, energy, and other areas as your body adjusts to the new diet. Getting into ketosis and putting your body into fat-burning mode can aid in weight loss and usually allows dieters to lose weight quickly.

4. Will the Carnivore Diet Cause Deficiencies in Nutrients?

An all-meat diet will not result in nutrient deficiencies if you vary your low-carb diet. You still need a lot of minerals and vitamins for your immune and digestive systems, but by including fish and shellfish on your carnivore diet food list, you can get these nutrients while avoiding stomach problems.

5. How Long Will It Take to Adapt to the Carnivore Diet?

It takes about a week to adjust to the carnivorous diet and enter full ketosis. Depending on how disciplined you are and how much you exercise, this could take up to two weeks.

6. Does a Carnivore Diet Put One in Ketosis?

The carnivore diet usually gets you into ketosis in 5 to 10 days. A carnivorous lifestyle, such as the ketogenic diet, eliminates almost all carb intake, leaving your body more reliant on fat and protein for energy.

7. Is a Carnivore Diet Expensive?

The carnivorous diet is undoubtedly expensive, but there are excellent ways to cut costs. You can still eat grass-fed beef daily if you choose cheaper cuts.

8. Does a Carnivore Diet Improves Testosterone?

Research on high-fat and low-fiber consumption shows that the carnivore diet can boost testosterone levels. However, remember that other health issues will also impact your testosterone levels.

9. How Long Will It Take For a Carnivore Diet to Work?

Everyone is different regarding adopting the carnivore diet and reaping the fantastic benefits. Some people see results in days, while others may take years to recover from physical trauma. Most people have fully adjusted and are reaping the benefits of the carnivorous diet after six months.

10. Any Difference Between the Keto and Carnivore Diets?

The main difference between the ketogenic and carnivore diets is that the keto diet allows certain carbs/fiber/plant-based meals while the carnivore diet does not. The keto diet allows for consuming berries, nuts, and other low-carb plant foods. On the other hand, the carnivore diet prohibits any animal-derived items.

How to Overcome Common Challenges

For many years, studies have linked red meat diets to cardiovascular disease, diabetes, and other negative side effects.

This all-meat diet is one of the most limited options.

Adaptation Period Symptoms

It will take some time for your body to adjust to the nutritional, hormonal, and intestinal changes caused by the complete elimination of most food categories.

Throughout the adaptation phase, many unfavorable symptoms and side effects will occur.

Nausea and flu are the most common transient side effects, but they usually go away after 2-4 weeks. Cognitive fog, impatience, cravings, poor attention, and headaches are other symptoms to expect during the adjustment period.

Tips for Staying Motivated and On Track

Consume plenty of water. Here are two additional easy strategies to help lessen, if not eliminate, the majority of your discomfort while you adjust to the carnivorous diet:

Consuming More Meat

A carnivore diet is often high in fat and protein, so you'll feel full for a long time. This may deceive you into eating very little, and therein lies the problem.

One of the main reasons 'carnivores' suffer is that they eat infrequently. It is common to experience extreme hunger during the first few weeks; the last thing you want to do is ignore it.

To satisfy your hunger, eat more meat or higher-quality cuts. Instead of worrying about gaining weight, figure out how many calories you need and use that number to determine food portions.

Supplements for Electrolyte Support

When glycogen stores are broken down to release energy, you will lose weight in the first few days—weight loss is natural when you don't eat carbohydrates. This process removes a significant amount of water and sodium, chloride, potassium, and magnesium, all of which must be replaced. But how precisely? Increase your salt intake.

Drink meaty bone broth to replenish water and add salt and potassium, which will help alleviate some of the discomfort. If this doesn't work, you may need an electrolyte supplement to mineralize yourself.

Additional tablets are especially important if magnesium or potassium are depleted. The optimum daily values for various deficiencies are 2-7g sodium, 0.25-0.5g magnesium, and 0.5-3.5g potassium.

Chapter 10: Inspiring Stories from Real-Life Carnivore Dieters

Denise – COVID Survivor

Denise uses the Carnivore Diet to lose weight while improving her digestion and mental health.

She was a COVID ventilator survivor who began the carnivore diet shortly after being released in January 2022. She contracted COVID in early November 2021 and was still not feeling well after ten days. She took Ivermectin and Z-pac but was unable to obtain Hydroxyclorequin. After ten days of quarantine, she was placed on a ventilator and told she would die if she did not. After 15 days, she was removed from the vent and survived.

She was almost unable to do anything after that.

She was eager to begin the diet but was unsure if it was safe while on blood thinners. She had been taking Eliquis since she was discharged from the hospital. She had been on a diet for 11 months and had not gained any weight since returning home from the hospital. Her mood and mental clarity had improved. She had more energy, no stomach or bloating issues, her skin looked great, and her hair was growing nicely. In August 2022, her A1C level was 5.2.

The hardest part for her was being unable to eat sweets or bread. She quickly lost her desire for junk food and began craving steak, ground beef, bacon, and eggs. Her appetite has shrunk to the point where she only eats one meal per day on most days. Her hunger was manageable, and she only ate when she became hungry. The author lost weight thanks to the carnivore diet, but they also lost muscle mass.

The Buff Dudes

Hudson and Brandon White, dubbed the Buff Dudes, have taken on several challenges they have shared with their over 2 million YouTube followers. They only recently revealed what life is like on a carnivorous diet.

Both tried the routine for 30 days, recorded how they felt, and uploaded it to YouTube in their usual hilarious style.

The White brothers were astounded to discover that when they eliminated carbohydrates from their diet, their energy levels did not drop. They appreciated that eating carnivorous made them pay close attention to what they ate. They also discovered that it did not affect their workouts.

Both, however, rated it a "no flex" because they enjoy eating various foods. In other words, it's not for everyone.

Chris and Mark Bell

Carnivorous eating is a family tradition, especially for brothers Mark and Chris Bell.

Chris was an early proponent of the carnivore diet, telling onnit.com that he started in 1994 when he lost 20 pounds in two weeks by eating only red meat and water. He continued for another two years after that, and after a brief hiatus, he resumed in January 2018 while working on his documentary, The War on Carbs.

Chris Bell admits to eating fruit when hungry, but he's a carnivore 99 percent of the time.

Powerlifter Mark "The Meathead Millionaire" Bell is a big fan of the carnivorous diet. He's not as strict as his brother, but following him on Instagram may help you learn more about him.

Mikhaila and Jordan Peterson

Mikhaila may be the first carnivore diet influencer, and the father-daughter duo may be the most well-known name to adopt the carnivore diet. Mikhaila has updated her health journey by posting images of those who have followed her advice and succeeded with the diet Instagram. She created "The Lion Diet," which claims to improve people's health by eating only meat.

Mikhaila had several health issues as a child, and she only found relief when she eliminated all foods other than animal products from her diet.

Jordan Peterson, a renowned political speaker and psychologist, told Rogan on his podcast that the diet helped him overcome lifelong ailments such as depression, stomach acid, and mood swings.

There are no signs that either will give up the diet anytime soon.

Conclusion and Final Thoughts

The carnivore diet is popular, but it is a severely restricted diet with no scientific backing. It may produce immediate results, such as weight loss, but many people will likely find it difficult to maintain it long-term.

Carnivores eat only meat, fish, eggs, and a small amount of low-lactose dairy. It is thought to aid in weight loss and various health conditions, but no solid research supports these claims. Furthermore, it is high in fat and salt, deficient in fiber and important plant chemicals, and difficult to maintain over time.

You should avoid this or any other fad diet if you have a history of disordered eating. Anyone suffering from a chronic illness, such as diabetes or heart disease, should consult their doctor before embarking on an extreme diet like this. Finally, if you have kidney disease, you should avoid eating meat.

Reflections on the Carnivore Diet and Lifestyle

Despite a lack of research, the benefits of a carnivore diet can be supported by current knowledge. The carnivore diet, with its high protein content and almost no carbohydrates, is arguably the most satiating, least calorie-dense diet a person could eat, making it suitable for long-term caloric restriction. Unsurprisingly, newcomers to the carnivorous diet benefit from rapid weight loss.

If a person reports relief from a carnivorous diet, especially in severe cases like Mikhaila Peterson's, it would be difficult to suggest that they return to their misery. However, given the potentially dangerous consequences of avoiding plant fiber, it's critical to investigate the mechanisms underlying the carnivore diet to achieve the same result more safely.

According to JAMA's large association study, eating meat does not increase the risk of premature death unless combined with at least one risky lifestyle factor.

Obesity, lack of physical activity, alcohol abuse, and cigarette smoking, among other unhealthy lifestyle habits, will turn your meat into a liability.

The Future of Carnivore Cuisine

Bitcoin enthusiasts and tech-savvy libertarians are particularly fond of the carnivorous diet.

More meat, milk, and eggs have been consumed globally in recent decades than ever before. Our lifestyle choices have an impact on our health, the welfare of animals, and the environment. What is causing the increase? And how will patterns shift in the coming decades?

A variety of factors may influence demand. The most straightforward models are human population, income, and income elasticity. Economists use simulations to assess the effects of policies. By adjusting income growth while holding other variables constant, they can forecast how our incomes affect our diets.

This study does just that, and the models used by the researchers provide a rough picture of animal product consumption in 2050. The average person will consume 14% more calories than they do now. The world will eat 38% more meat than it does now. South Asia and Sub-Saharan Africa will see the greatest increases in consumption. People in prosperous countries may eventually eat less than they do now if global income elasticities fall.

Slower-than-expected global income growth will reduce consumption in impoverished countries while increasing consumption in affluent countries compared to a typical growth scenario.

Final Recommendations and Encouragement

The all-meat or carnivore diet is gaining popularity on social media platforms like TikTok. Leave it to TikTok to start 2023 with a fiery debate. Many people have posted recipes, weekly meals, and useful information under the hashtag #allmeatdiet, which has received over 1 million views.

No evidence exists that an all-meat diet heals juvenile rheumatoid arthritis, and no treatment exists. However, stories like Jordan Peterson's may provide some hope for some people suffering from a condition or persistent symptoms without a diagnosis or treatment plan.

"We don't have a good treatment or explanation for everything that happens to us," says Dr. Konstantinos Spaniolas, chief of the division of bariatric, foregut, and advanced GI surgery at Stony Brook Medicine. "People strive to find a diet that will assist them in managing their disease; it represents a ray of hope for individuals."

Manufactured by Amazon.ca
Bolton, ON